Home
WATER &
MOISTURE
Problems

Home
WATER &
MOISTURE
Problems

Including wet basements, roof leaks, moisture and humidity problems, and plumbing problems

GARY BRANSON

KEY PORTER BOOKS

National Library of Canada Cataloguing in Publication

Branson, Gary D.
    The complete guide to solving home water & moisture problems / Gary Branson.

Includes index.
ISBN 1-55263-228-8

    1. Dampness in buildings—Amateurs' manuals. 2. Drainage, House—Amateurs' manuals. 3. Dwellings—Maintenance and repair—Amateurs' manuals. 4. Waterproofing—Amateurs' manuals. I. Title.

TH9031.B73 2003   693.8'92   C2003-900330-2

THE CANADA COUNCIL | LE CONSEIL DES ARTS
FOR THE ARTS | DU CANADA
SINCE 1957 | DEPUIS 1957

ONTARIO ARTS COUNCIL
CONSEIL DES ARTS DE L'ONTARIO

The publisher gratefully acknowledges the support of the Canada Council for the Arts and the Ontario Arts Council for its publishing program.

We acknowledge the financial support of the Government of Canada through the Book Publishing Industry Development Program (BPIDP) for our publishing activities.

Key Porter Books Limited
70 The Esplanade
Toronto, Ontario
Canada M5E 1R2

www.keyporter.com

Design: Peter Maher
Electronic formatting: Jean Peters

Printed and bound in Canada

03 04 05 06 07 5 4 3 2 1

CONTENTS

Introduction

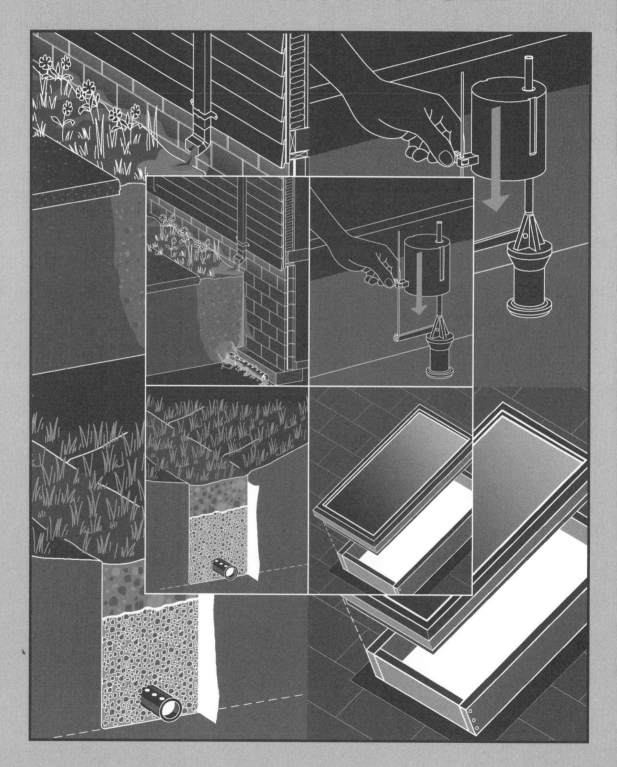

I am a former contractor, and was for ten years senior editor of *Family Handyman* magazine. One of my editorial duties was to answer readers' questions, 60 percent of which involved water problems: wet basements, leaking roofs or plumbing, mold and mildew, and excess moisture or humidity.

Further research reinforced my opinion that this subject required a book. For example, in *The Complete Book of Home Inspection,* author Norman Becker, a plant engineer, states that the fourth most common house problem is wet basements. According to Becker, 50 percent of houses with basements have basement water problems. The eighth most common problem, damaged or missing roof gutters, affects 34 percent of all houses.

The University of Minnesota Department of Public Service echoes Becker's estimate that wet basements plague 50 percent of houses in Minnesota; in my own work as a housing inspector, 75 percent of queries from clients have involved basement water problems. In a press release the American Society of Home Inspectors (ASHI) named wet basements as the problem most often found by ASHI inspectors.

An increasingly common problem concerns home humidity and its attendant problems. To reduce air infiltration and conserve energy, many current building codes call for tight construction, including full wall and ceiling vapor retarders. This requirement helps improve the energy efficiency of the house, but the lack of air entry may also raise indoor humidity levels to unacceptable or even damaging levels. The result can be a multitude of problems, including wood rot, rust and corrosion of the furnace or other steel appliances, damage to the interior plaster or wallboard, peeling paint on both the interior and exterior of the house, ruined insulation, and mildew or mold and their attendant odors.

Other home water problems involve leaking roofs or leaking plumbing, and an increasing concern for water conservation. To answer those concerns, and to offer solutions, I've written this book.

One word of caution. Most of the advice offered in this book is aimed at moisture problems of houses in geographical areas where there are four distinct seasons. Therefore, the advice and possible solutions given may not be applicable in all areas of the nation.

For example, the coastal states from the Gulf of Mexico to the Virginias have warm temperatures and high humidity year-round. In these areas, where air conditioning may keep interior house temperatures lower than outdoor temperatures, the "cold side of the wall" will be the *interior* side. Any vapor barrier should be placed between the wall sheathing and exterior siding, rather than between the wallboard and the studs as is usually recommended. Also, in a narrow band just above these coastal states the weather and humidity are such that *no* vapor barrier is recommended.

Another example is the recommendations for venting of attics or crawl spaces. In cooler climates it is necessary to vent the moisture from the crawl space to the drier air outside. But in warm, humid climates the exterior air may carry more moisture than interior or crawl space air, so ventilation may *add* moisture to these areas and compound any moisture problems.

Building codes and conventional wisdom thus will vary according to geographical region, and readers are cautioned always to follow local building codes, consult local inspectors, and follow the time-tested customs for building in their particular climate.

PART I

BASEMENTS

CHAPTER 1

Wet Basements

In houses with basements, the single most commonly reported problem is a wet basement. Wet basements result from two possible sources of water: ground water (the rain and snow that falls on a property) or a high water table. However, according to estimates from the National Association of Home Builders, 95 percent of basement water problems are simply due to the entry into the basement of ground water from rain and snow. Only 5 percent of wet basements are caused by a high water level in the soil.

Because there is nothing the homeowner can do to change the water table, a complex and expensive system of trenches, pipes, and sump pumps is the only cure for removing water that enters from a high water table. But, as we will see, the odds are great that the homeowner can cure the wet basement problem by attacking the problem of ground water entry. This cure may be accomplished by adding or improving a rain gutter system to deliver roof water away from the house, by correcting the slope or grade of the land adjacent to the house so that water will be diverted and will flow quickly away from the basement, or by patching basement cracks and

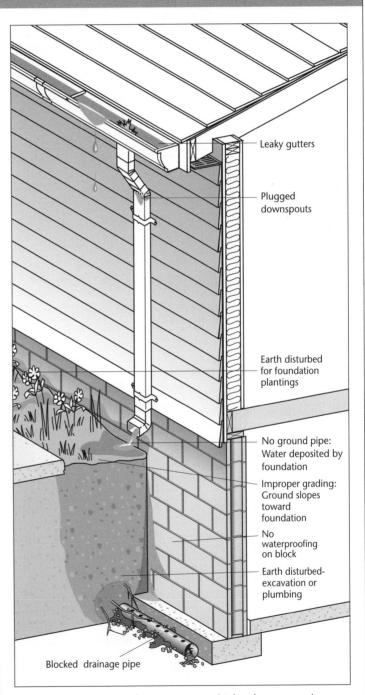

Common Sources of Wet Basements

Leaky gutters

Plugged downspouts

Earth disturbed for foundation plantings

No ground pipe: Water deposited by foundation

Improper grading: Ground slopes toward foundation

No waterproofing on block

Earth disturbed- excavation or plumbing

Blocked drainage pipe

Poor water management due to common mistakes shown, are primary cause of wet basements.

Water Table

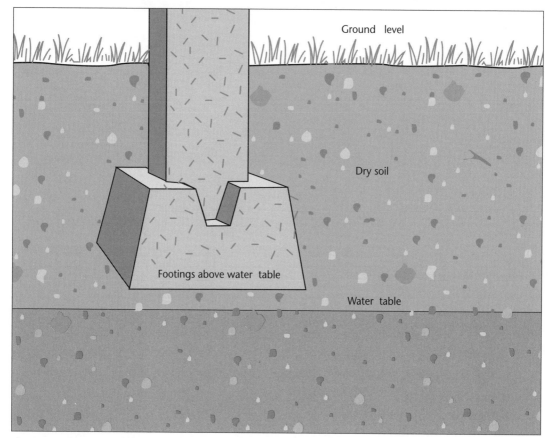

Ground level

Dry soil

Footings above water table

Water table

The water table is the depth at which the soil is always wet. Call your building department to learn the water table depth in your area.

applying one or more coats of a waterproofing material to the interior side of the basement's concrete walls. To ensure a permanent cure for wet basement problems, any solution should include all three of the above steps: adding or improving roof gutters, correcting any grade problems, and waterproofing the basement walls.

UNDERSTANDING THE WATER TABLE

Professional waterproofers often cite a high water table as the probable source for basement water problems. Waterproofers stand to profit from this diagnosis; blaming a high water table means the problem is beyond any self-help remedy and professionals will have to take extensive and expensive steps to cure the problem.

These steps may include excavation and/or trenching, hauling in gravel fill to build leach beds (trenches filled with gravel to disperse the water via ground absorption and evaporation), installing perforated drain pipes and a sump pump, and application of both interior and exterior waterproof coatings to the basement walls. These remedies could easily occupy a work crew for several days and justify a bill of thou-

Setting Excavated Soil

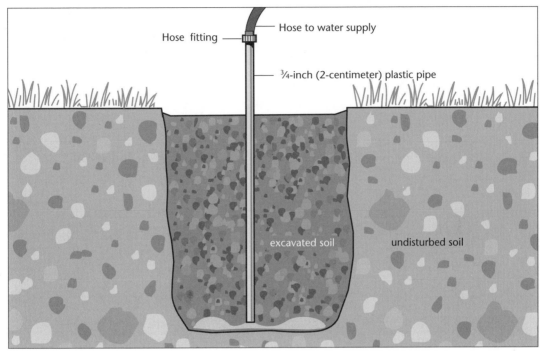

Hose to water supply

Hose fitting

¾-inch (2-centimeter) plastic pipe

excavated soil

undisturbed soil

To settle soil in a trench, attach a hose to an 8-foot (2.5-meter) plastic pipe. Push the pipe down to the bottom of the excavation and turn on the water. The water will force out air pockets and dissolve clumps of soil. As the fill dirt settles, raise the pipe upwards.

sands of dollars. However, eliminating ground water problems can be a do-it-yourself job that will offer a relatively inexpensive solution for the majority of wet basements.

Before investigating the source of a basement water problem I should define the term "water table." The water table is the depth at which the earth is permanently saturated with water. If you are so unlucky as to have a basement that penetrates into this continually wet soil, you must install drain pipes (either inside or outside the basement footings) and a sump pump to collect the water and move it away from the basement footings and floors.

Before assuming a high water table and calling a professional waterproofing company, consult experts to learn the level of the water table in your area. Your local building inspector can provide free information about the depth of the water table. For example, a call to the author's city building inspector might reveal that the water table in your area is at a depth of 17 feet (5 meters).

Because the basement penetrates less than 8 feet (2.5 meters) into the ground, I can assume that the water table begins some 9 feet (2.75 meters) below the basement floor, so it is obvious that there can be no water entry from the water table.

Another approach would be to consult excavating contractors who work in the area. These contractors dig basements and install utility piping such as water and sewer lines all over the community, and they can provide expert advice concerning the local water table.

Basement Construction for Wet Soil

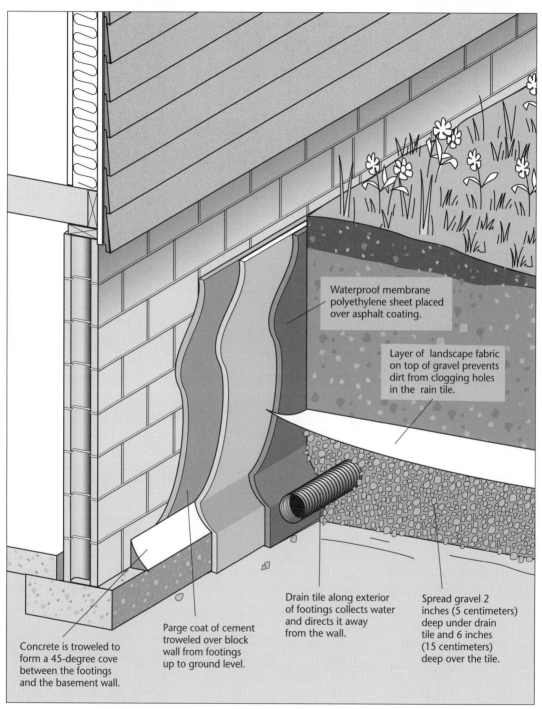

Waterproof membrane polyethylene sheet placed over asphalt coating.

Layer of landscape fabric on top of gravel prevents dirt from clogging holes in the rain tile.

Concrete is troweled to form a 45-degree cove between the footings and the basement wall.

Parge coat of cement troweled over block wall from footings up to ground level.

Drain tile along exterior of footings collects water and directs it away from the wall.

Spread gravel 2 inches (5 centimeters) deep under drain tile and 6 inches (15 centimeters) deep over the tile.

Basement construction varies depending on the type of soil. Check with building department for the code in your area.

Excavating contractors will have firsthand knowledge of any water table problems or underground springs in the area.

After checking with building inspectors and local excavators, consult the neighbors on all four sides of your house to learn if they, too, are having problems with water in the basement. The water table does not vary widely over a small area, i.e., from lot to lot. If you alone have a serious basement water problem while neighboring basements are dry, you can assume that the problem is not with the water table but is due strictly to runoff from surface water.

Be aware, however, that if a cluster of neighboring houses that historically have had dry basements suddenly develop wet basements, the problem is not with the water table. For example, I know of one neighborhood in which the basements had been dry for decades. When municipal sewer improvements were done, with extensive new trenching and soil disturbance, all the houses in an entire neighborhood suddenly developed basement water problems. What was the water source? The disturbed soil had allowed rain to percolate in and run through all the pipe trenches. Those excavations included a new trench run-

ning from the main sewer route up to the basement of each house, a natural avenue through which surface water could flow. The epidemic of wet basements was caused by the sewer excavations, and the basement water problems were not eliminated until the fill dirt settled in the trenches, so that ground water could no longer penetrate the soil.

Some texts maintain that the depth of the water table varies with the seasons, and with the amount of rainfall. It is obviously true that the amount of water present in the upper levels of the soil varies with the wet and dry seasons, but this is still considered a surface water problem. The true water table, the point at which water is always present in the soil, is constant and does not depend on the seasons. In wet weather you are simply dealing with more surface water.

Finally, modern building codes do not permit contractors to build basements in areas where the water table is high. In some cases you may be permitted to build, but without a basement, on a slab on grade. Decades ago, building codes were not as strict, so houses that are more than 30 years old may have been built on a lot with a high water table. But if your house was built in the last two or three decades you

can be reasonably sure that a high water table is not the problem. Again, your building inspector will be able to advise you whether or not the water table may be the source of basement water.

If inspectors and contractors respond that the water table in your area is an unlikely source of basement water problems, you can assume that the basement water problem is from surface water. A little detective work will help you locate the route through which water is entering your basement so you can eliminate any problems.

MANAGING WATER

To ensure good drainage and a dry basement, consider the total volume of water that you must manage or divert from the basement perimeter. For example, consider a house built on a city lot that is 75 feet wide and 125 feet deep (23 meters by 38 meters), or a total of 9,375 square feet (874 square meters). If we multiply 9,375 square feet by 144 (square inches per square foot) (or 874 square meters by 10,000 centimeters per square meter) we have 1,350,000 square inches (8,740,000 square centimeters). A rainfall of 1 inch (2.5 centimeters) would mean that we have 1,350,000 *cubic*

Mortar Joints

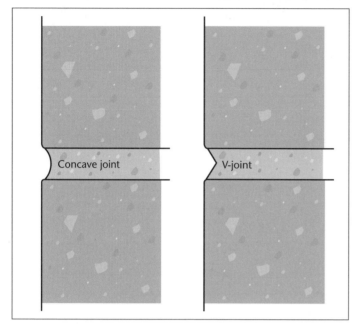

Minor details such as tooling masonry joints can help waterproof a foundation wall. Masons use special tools to make the joints shown. Tooling the joints compresses the mortar, eliminates bubbles, and makes joints dense and water-tight.

inches (8,740,000 cubic centimeters) of water. If we divide 1,350,000 by 231 (the number of cubic inches in a gallon of water) 3,785 milliliters/gallon/3,788 liters, we realize that 5,844 gallons (22,119 liters) of water is dropped by a 1-inch (2.5 centimeters) rainfall on this lot. A 2-inch (5- centimeters) rain would mean dealing with 11,688 gallons (44,138 liters) of water in one rainstorm—enough water to fill several swimming pools. Water naturally flows downhill, and for water that reaches the perimeter of the foundation, downhill means

into the basement. You thus must manage the water that falls on the entire lot so that it is diverted or deposited at least 5 to 10 feet (1.5 to 3 meters) from the foundation wall. If your landscaping is poorly done, much of that water can find its way into your basement.

If you make your inspection during a rain, you can see which way the water runoff flows, so it is wise to do your detective work when it is raining. Stand in your back yard. Note which way the lot slopes. If the lot is properly graded, most of the water will find its way to curbside, and

be carried away by storm drains. If you live near a pond or running stream, the water runoff may be toward these bodies of water.

If standing in your back yard is like standing in an arena, with all sides of the grade sloping toward your foundation, you may have to call in an engineer to create a new landscape plan. The engineer will be able to assess the problem and order a new survey, then have an excavating contractor regrade the property. This extensive remedy is rarely needed for existing houses, because establishing proper grade and water runoff should have been done, and usually is done, during the construction process.

Also, be aware that the most critical portion of your lawn is the 10-foot (3-meter) strip on all sides and immediately adjacent to your house. A lot may have a considerable slope or even a hill sloping toward the house, but if the grade slopes away from your basement walls so that water cannot stand or puddle within 10 feet (3-meters) of the basement, the basement will remain dry.

So, to maintain a dry basement you must be especially careful to divert all the water that (1) falls on the roof of the house, as well as (2) the water that falls on the 10-foot-wide (3-meter-wide) strip of lawn immediately

Sump Pump

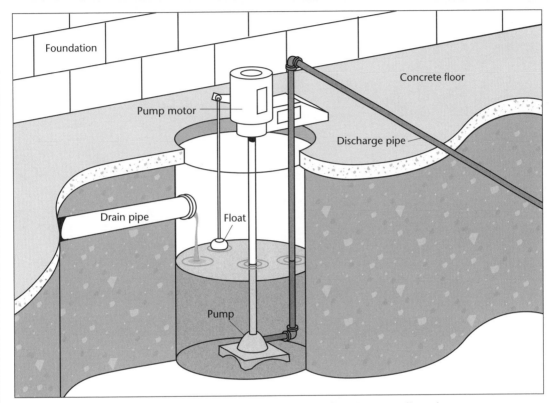

Foundation

Concrete floor

Pump motor

Discharge pipe

Drain pipe

Float

Pump

Foundation perimeter drain pipe carries water into the sump; pump directs water to disposal.

adjacent to the house on all of its four sides. I chose the 10-foot- (3-meter) width because any water that falls and puddles within 10 feet (3 meters) of the house perimeter may either run back toward the basement or may seep through light (sandy or loam) soil to reach the basement, where it may cause a problem.

Obviously, if even a small portion of ground water finds its way back to the basement, you can have a serious basement water problem. To avoid any prob-lems with water or humidity in the basement, you must formulate a plan to divert all this water away from the basement walls. First, you must solve the problem of disposing of the roof water, then establish a proper slope or grade to carry away the water that falls upon the lawn.

RAIN GUTTERS

When building a house, the contractor must assess the need for rain gutters to han-dle the roof water. Points to consider include the size of the roof, the width of roof overhangs or soffits at the eaves, the grade or lay and slope of the lawn, whether the house has a basement, and the type of soil. All these factors can affect water runoff and disposal. The builder will make an edu-cated guess on whether the water disposal is sufficient to ensure a dry basement with-out gutters. Because gutters can add hundreds or even thousands of dollars to the cost of the house, the builder may err in the direction of

Avoid Gutter Plugs

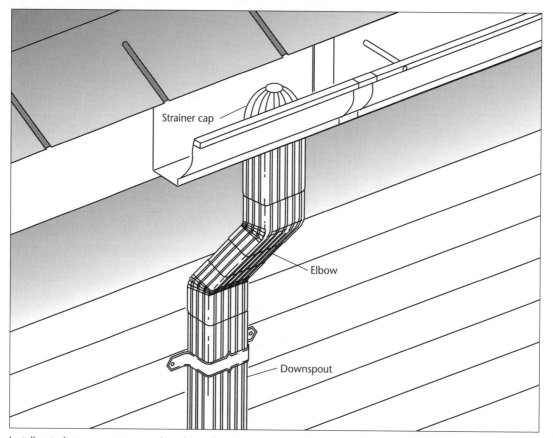

Strainer cap

Elbow

Downspout

Install a strainer cap, gutter guard mesh, or clog-free gutters to eliminate problems with gutter debris.

his own best interests, and decide not to add rain gutters to the house.

Since World War II, the trend in residential building has been to have wider soffits (i.e., 3 to 4 feet [1 to 1.2 meters] of roof overhang) at the eaves, and to eliminate rain gutters. The wider soffits let the roof water run off the roof and fall to earth at a greater distance from the foundation or basement walls, where a proper grade or slope to the lawn will per-mit the water to run quickly away from the foundation.

Many homeowners who have problems with a wet basement will refuse to add rain gutters on the theory that if the builder did not install them, they must not be needed. Be aware that the builder just made an edu-cated guess that the house would function without gut-ters. However, he or she may have miscalculated, so if water problems do develop, consider adding rain gutters to guarantee the proper disposal of roof water to the ground, then correct the grade to ensure runoff.

Gutters: D-I-Y or Pro Installation?

To ensure that your house has a well-engineered gutter system, hire a gutter contractor rather than doing the work yourself. Gutters are offered in a variety of sizes, and the size chosen depends on the size of the roof in square feet, i.e., the volume

Splash Block

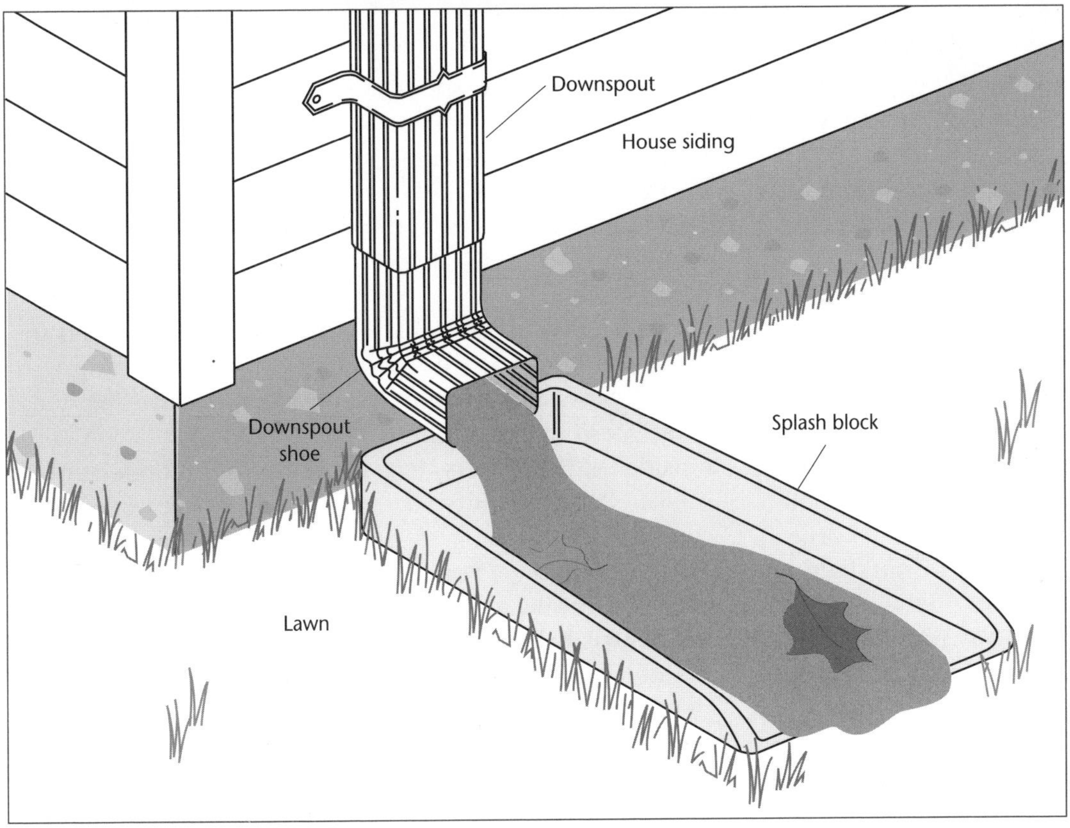

Downspout

House siding

Downspout shoe

Splash block

Lawn

A splash block will prevent soil erosion and divert water at the ground. If space permits, a 6-foot (2 meter) long ground pipe is a better solution.

of water that must be handled by the gutters. The gutters also must have a continuous slope toward the downspouts. The size, number, and position of the downspouts must be adequate to quickly carry the water from the gutters to the ground, then to an area that will ensure that there will be quick runoff with no pooling or puddling of the water near the foundation. Once the downspouts have delivered the water to ground

level, the ground pipes must be long enough to deliver the water well away—at least 6 feet (2 meters), though more is better—from the foundation. Have a respected professional plan and install the gutter system.

When consulting a professional gutter contractor, trust his or her advice. Unfortunately, many homeowners will reject the pro's advice, fearing that gutter components will detract from the appearance of the

house. I've seen large houses with only four downspouts, one at each of the four corners of the house, to carry the water from the gutters to the ground. The length of the gutter run may call for extra downspouts in the center of the run, but because they occur at the midpoint of the house, homeowners may reject them as being unsightly. The inadequate downspouts cannot handle the volume of water collected by the gutters, so the gutters fill and overflow along their length. When gutters drop water at the roof edge, rather than delivering it to a diversion point at ground level, water enters the basement as if there were no gutters at all.

The most common mistake that homeowners make with gutters is to neglect or even to eliminate the ground pipes that carry the water away from the foundation. While inspecting wet basements I have found that most downspouts simply dump the water in a pool within 1 or 2 feet (.3 or .6 meters) of the foundation. The water often will then find its way into the basement, rather than flowing away from the foundation.

INSPECTING THE GUTTERS

If your house has gutters, conduct a complete inspection of the gutter system. The best time to do this is during a moderate to heavy rain, when water is present and you can follow the disposal route from roof to ground level, and then away from the foundation. To inspect the rain gutters without climbing, use a pair of binoculars to get an up-close view of all the components.

The next step is to inspect the gutters at the roof edge when rain stops. You can do this from the roof, or from ground level if you prefer. Be aware, however, that even a handful of leaves or debris may clog the gutters at the point where they enter the downspouts, so to perform a complete inspection you must position yourself on the roof or on a ladder high enough to visually inspect the entire gutter system.

Be sure the gutters are clean and free of any debris such as leaves, limbs, and twigs. Stain marks on the outsides of the gutters clearly indicate that the gutter system is overflowing along its length. If your gutters clog and overflow frequently, have a professional trim any nearby trees to remove overhanging limbs and deadwood to reduce future debris buildup.

When you are sure the gutters are clean, check the gutter joints to be sure they are not leaking water. Check also to be sure the gutters are large enough to handle the heaviest rainfall without overflowing.

Check the downspouts that carry the water from the gutters to the ground. Be sure the downspouts are open so water can flow freely to ground level. If the downspouts are blocked with leaves, push the nozzle of a garden hose into the downspout and flush out the debris with water pressure.

Now that the roof water can travel to ground level, what will you do with it? Keep in mind that a 1-inch (2.5 centimeter) rainfall will deposit nearly 1,000 gallons (3,785 liters) of water on a 1,500 square foot (139 square meter) roof. A gutter system serving a roof of this size will have need four to six downspouts to carry water from the gutters to ground level. Assuming the water is equally diverted, this means that between 166 gallons (628 liters) and 250 gallons (946 liters) of water will fall to the ground through each downspout. To ensure that the basement stays dry, install longer ground pipes—the pipes at the bottom of the downspouts—so that the water is diverted at least 10 feet (3 meters) from the foundation when it reaches the ground.

While it is raining, notice how the water exits from the downspouts and flows into the ground pipes. How far away from the foundation is the point at which the water is deposited? What is the water's path as it flows from the end of the ground pipes? Does the water continue to flow away from the house foundation, or does it run back toward it? Any water that lies in pools or runs back toward the basement foundation is a potential problem.

Be especially careful when checking ground pipes that terminate on a sidewalk, driveway, or patio. Water that is deposited on concrete slabs that are flat, or slope slightly toward the foundation, often will run back toward the house and into the basement. Any concrete or asphalt slabs that are adjacent to the foundation must be sloped so that water runs away from the foundation.

Ground pipes should never terminate in cultivated areas such as flower beds, where the soil is kept loosened and is therefore very absorbent. Large amounts of water will soak through this loose soil and reach the basement wall. The ground pipes must be long enough to deliver the water onto a grassy surface, or onto a sloping concrete slab, such as a driveway, where it will run away from the basement wall.

If you inspect the system during a rainfall, you will be able to track the water flow through the gutter system, onto a paved or grassy area, and down the lawn to the street gutters and storm drains, or to a rain collection basin such as a pond or stream.

GRADING THE BASEMENT PERIMETER

To reduce basement water problems, the most important portion of the lot to be graded is the lawn that is within 10 feet (3 meters) of the basement wall or foundation. If this critical area is properly graded, so that no water can pool within 10 feet (3 meters) of the basement, the water will not soak back through the soil and enter the basement.

Expert advice varies regarding the slope needed around the basement to prevent water entry. For

Basement Construction Wet Soil

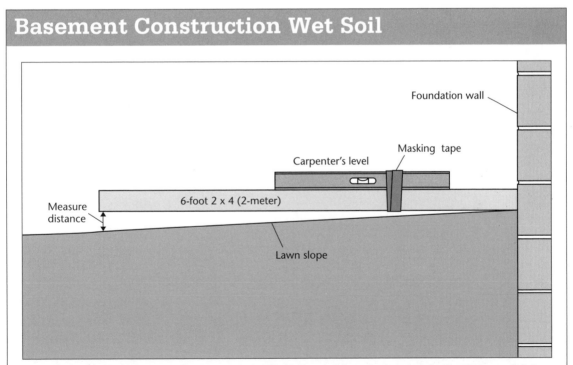

To check the grade of your lawn, place one end of a 6-foot (2-meter) long 2 x 4 against the foundation wall. Raise the outer end of the 2 x 4 until the 2 x 4 is level. Measure the distance between the lawn and the bottom edge of the 2 x 4: if less than 3 inches (7.5 centimeters), add soil at the foundation wall to increase the slope.

Pro Transit

A transit is a telescope mounted on a tripod. The legs adjust so the unit can be leveled, and a plumb bob is hung from under the unit. The surveyor looks through an eyepiece to sight an oversized ruler at a distant point.

example, a major home inspection company, HouseMaster of America, recommends that the slope or grade of the soil should be 3 inches per foot for the first 3 feet (7.5 centimeters per 0.3 meters for the first meter), or a 15-degree angle. But water can soak a long distance in very loose or sandy soil, so I prefer to extend the slope so it drops 1 inch or more per foot of run (2.5 centimeters per 30 centimeters of run), for a distance of 10 feet (3 meters) away from the basement wall. This means that the grade from the basement wall outward would have a slope of

Using a Transit

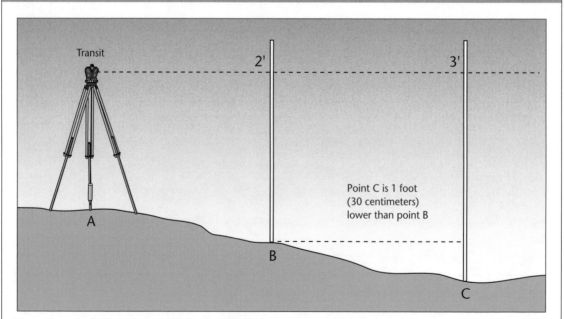

Transit

2'   3'

Point C is 1 foot (30 centimeters) lower than point B

A

B

C

The surveyor looks through the optical unit while a helper moves a ruled stake to various points. The surveyor reads the markings on the stake to determine the slope of the land.

10 inches in 10 feet (25 centimeters in 3 meters).

To check your grade or slope, use a 6-foot (2-meter) straight edge such as a straight 2 × 4. With the 2 × 4 sitting on its narrow edge, use masking tape to tape a 24-inch (50-centimeter) carpenter's level to the top of the 2 × 4.

Now, set the 2 × 4 on the ground with one end against the wall. Does the 2 × 4 touch the ground along its entire length, or are there ridges and dips along the bottom edge? The slope should be continuous, without any low spots or dips where water can puddle and soak back to the basement wall. If the slope is not continuous, fill the low spots with dirt to eliminate the possibility of water puddling.

To check the grade, leave the 2 × 4 end that is against the basement wall sitting on the ground. Lift the outside end of the 2 × 4 until the bubble is centered in the level. Now use a ruler or measuring tape to measure the distance from the ground up to the bottom edge of the 2 × 4. If the straight edge is 10 feet (3 meters) long, the distance should measure 10 inches (25 centimeters). If the slope is less, add dirt and contour it so the slope is 10 inches (25 centimeters) over 10 feet (3 meters) of run.

Keep in mind that any improvement in the slope of the lawn is better than none at all, and even a slope of ½ inch (1 centimeters) per foot of run will permit water to run away, providing the soil is not cultivated as it would be in a flower bed.

However, before adding soil, check the distance from the bottom edge of the exterior wall siding down to the ground. You should maintain a distance of at least 8 inches (20 centimeters)—more distance is preferable, especially in snow country—between the ground and the bottom edge of the siding. If you add enough dirt at the basement wall to raise the slope to 1 inch (2.5 centimeters) of drop per foot of run, can you maintain at least 8 inches (20 centimeters) of space between the bottom of the siding and the ground?

If you cannot add more dirt at the basement wall, you can call in a landscape contractor to use a device called a transit to accurately shoot or determine a grade. He or she will drive grade stakes, then use a small tractor to cut away the soil so the grade slopes away from the basement wall. This will leave a slight drainage ditch, called a swale, 10 feet (3 meters) away from the basement wall. Water then cannot stand or puddle within 10 feet (3 meters) of the basement wall, which will ensure a dry basement. (See Chapter 2, Correcting the Grade.)

Correcting the Grade

In Chapter 1, Wet Basements, we discussed the roof gutter system, i.e., the means by which you direct the water from rain or snowmelt off the roof and deliver it to ground level. After inspecting the gutters, and checking that the ground pipes are delivering the water at least 10 feet (3 meters) away from the foundation wall, we must be sure that there is a continuous slope or grade to the lawn adjoining the house. If this slope or grade is properly maintained, so there is at least 1 inch (2.5 centimeters) of drop for each foot (0.3 meters) of run away from the basement foundation wall, the water will always run downhill—away from the basement—and will never cause basement water problems.

IMPROPER INITIAL GRADE

Grade problems can result from a number of factors. First, the builder/landscape contractor may have been careless in grading around the foundation or perhaps over the entire lot, and from the day the house was new there may have been little slope to direct the water away from the foundation. Water will always follow the laws of gravity, i.e., will run downhill, and if downhill means toward the founda-

tion, the result will be a basement water problem.

Again, keep in mind that a 1,500-square-foot (140-square-meter) roof catches 1,000 gallons (379 liters) of water in a 1-inch (2.5 centimeter) rain. Expressed another way, that is twenty 50-gallon (190-liter) barrels of water that, without proper gutters, will be deposited within a few feet of your basement wall or foundation. If you have a wet basement your gutter system should be upgraded so that it is adequate to manage and dispose of that large amount of water.

FOUNDATION PLANTINGS

In most cases, the builder has left the lot and lawn of the newly completed house with a slope or grade that will ensure that water will run away from the house. But often, the homeowner will act as his own landscaping expert and do his own foundation planting, thus disturbing the grade around the foundation. Keep in mind that soil that has never been disturbed will shed water rather than absorb it, but the soil around the basement was dug up and loosened during the basement excavation. After the basement was erected, the soil was backfilled, or pushed back against the basement walls. Given time, that backfill soil will settle and become

increasingly resistant to water penetration.

However, if homeowners plant foundation foliage such as shrubbery or flower beds, they will weed and cultivate the soil, keeping it constantly loosened so that it will absorb moisture. During planting or cultivation, the loose soil may also be raked and flattened, which will eliminate the grade or slope of the lawn. Because there is no grade to encourage water runoff, the water will puddle near the foundation and easily penetrate to footing levels via the excavated soil. The result will be a basement wall that leaks, often at the point where the concrete wall meets the concrete basement floor or slab.

If water appears to be soaking into the flower beds at the basement wall, and running into the basement, the first step must be to correct the grade. To do this, you may have to dig up and remove any foundation plantings, add soil at the wall, then grade the soil so that it slopes away from the house foundation. To learn how this is done, refer to Foundation Treatment illustration on page 26.

When a proper grade has been established, at least 1 inch (2.5 centimeters) per running foot (30 centimeters), you must choose between two options. The

Foundation Treatment

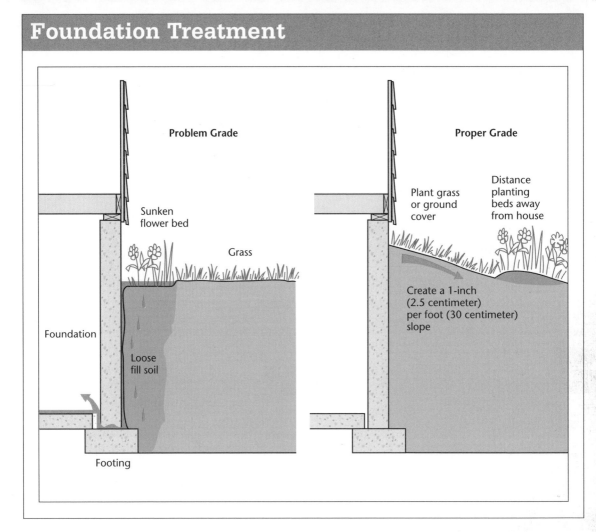

first and most effective option is to eliminate any foundation plantings. Because grass will shed water rather than absorb it, it is best to lay sod next to the foundation for at least 6 feet (2 meters) away from the house. Then reestablish the flower beds or shrubbery groupings in islands at least 6 feet (2 meters) away from the foundation. This may seem an unusual solution and unlikely to provide the desired curbside view.

However, island plantings are as attractive as foundation beds, and they ensure that water cannot penetrate loose soil and enter the basement.

One common misconception is that covering the planting area with plastic sheeting, then filling flower beds or planting areas with decorative rock or tree bark will help to solve a basement water problem. However, unless a proper grade is first established, neither the plastic sheeting, rock, or tree

bark present any barrier to water entry.

So, if you must have foundation plantings, first ensure that there is a proper grade or slope within the planting area, then install a plastic water barrier over the area of the planting beds.

Lay a sheet of 6 mil poly (plastic sheeting available at lumber yards or building centers) at least 6 feet (2 meters) wide, or as wide as the bed, over the properly graded soil. Secure the plastic sheeting in place by using an acoustic caulk or adhesive to seal the edge of the plastic sheet to the foundation. Acoustic caulk will adhere well to plastic vapor retarders—better than other caulks. It's stickier. Also, acoustic caulk stays flexible when it cures, while others harden and crack. Overlap any joints by at least 8 inches (20 centimeters), and seal the joints with caulk so the plastic sheeting presents an uninterrupted barrier to water entry. Then lay out the garden or shrubbery placement, and cut holes through the plastic sheeting where flowers or shrubs will be planted. These holes should be no larger than necessary to permit the planting, and should be limited to a maximum diameter of 12 inches (30 centimeters) or large enough to insert the root ball. Plant through the holes in the plastic. Then spread decorative stones, tree bark, or wood chips over the plastic. The decorative stones or chips will be attractive and will hold the plastic water barrier in place so the plastic sheeting will not become damaged or windblown. Use a hose or watering can to water the plants through the holes.

PAVED SLABS

Another critical portion of the lot is any area that is paved over concrete or asphalt. A grass turf will often absorb a 1-inch (2.5 centimeters) rain—or more,

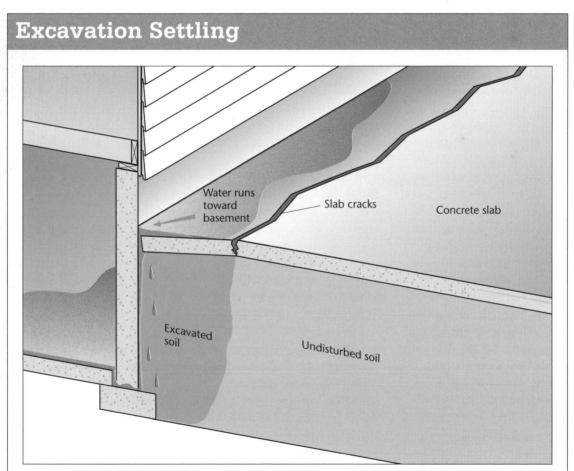

Excavation Settling

Water runs toward basement

Slab cracks

Concrete slab

Excavated soil

Undisturbed soil

Slabs poured over unsettled soil will crack as the soil settles. Do not pour concrete slabs such as drives or patios until the soil has settled.

depending on the type of soil—holding the water back so that it does not flow and cause a problem. But because no water is absorbed on a paved surface, all the water that falls on it must run off, and in many cases the direction of that flowing water is toward the basement.

How-to texts for homeowners often advise that when pouring a slab such as a patio or walk the forms must be level, but this is bad advice. Any paved slab near a structure should be formed and poured so that the finished slab will slope away from the basement area. Hundreds of gallons of water may fall on a large drive, walk, or patio, and this water must be diverted away from the house. If the poured slab is level, much of the water that falls upon it will flow toward the basement. It is absolutely critical that there be a slight slope away from the basement, especially for slabs that are immediately adjacent to the basement wall.

An inspection of any slab adjacent to a basement may reveal that the slab has sunk on the house side so the slab has tilted toward the basement. Because the soil is excavated when the basement is dug, then pushed back to fill the hole without sufficient tamping of the soil, the soil will eventually settle. As the soil settles near the house, the slab settles toward the basement. Then any water that falls on that slab will run into the basement. This settling of the slab is commonly seen on walks, porches and steps, patios, and garage aprons that have been poured on fill soil that is not compacted. Excavation Settling illustration on page 27.

To prevent slabs from settling or tilting toward the basement, it is important to take care at the time of construction. Any backfilled soil must be compacted or settled. One easy way to compact loose soil is to soak it with water. This process may require repeated soaking of the loose soil before the soil is finally compacted. As the water percolates into the loose soil, it displaces any air bubbles or voids so the soil is firmly compacted

To compact loose soil, contractors also may use mechanical compacting machines that tamp the soil with repeated blows. These machines can also be rented at most tool rental outlets. Choose either the water method or power tamping to compact soil, and never pour a concrete or asphalt slab over loose fill soil. If you use water to compact the soil, be sure to let the area dry before you pour a slab on top.

When pouring a new slab, set the concrete forms so there is sufficient grade or slope away from the foundation. This slope should be at least 2 inches (5 centimeters) over a 12-foot-wide (4-meter) patio or drive. If you begin with an initial slope of 2 inches (5 centimeters), you can still retain sufficient slope on the newly poured slab, even if the slab edge toward the basement wall settles slightly. Having a slope on the slab will also prevent water from standing, and ice from forming on the slab during winter.

When pouring a concrete slab adjacent to a basement wall, install an expansion strip at the juncture between the slab and the concrete wall. When the concrete has cured, keep the expansion strip joint caulked using acrylic latex caulk to prevent water entry between the slab and the wall. Because caulk weathers and cracks, you should inspect the joint in the spring and fall, and recaulk as needed to ensure the joint is watertight and will not permit water entry.

If you have an existing concrete slab that has tilted toward the basement, you may be able to correct the slab slope without breaking it out and starting over. A concrete raising system, called mudjacking, bores holes into the slab before pumping concrete into the holes and under the sunken slab, raising it into position. For a contractor who specializes in raising concrete, look in the Yellow Pages under Concrete Contractors.

Finally, gutter down-spouts and ground pipes should not deposit roof water directly on any slab that is adjacent to the basement wall, unless that slab has a pronounced slope away from the foundation. Where possible, position the ground pipes so that water is deposited on grassy turf, where it can be absorbed or will run off. Redirecting the water flow may be as simple as replacing the ground pipe angle so water is deposited parallel to but at a distance from the wall, rather than being deposited directly in front of the wall.

LOT DRAINAGE

On a grassy lot, the turf and topsoil will absorb a great deal of water before being saturated, so the water will not run off and create a problem. Below the topsoil, the ability of soil to absorb water depends on the type of soil. Loose loam or sandy soil will absorb water easily, while heavy black or clay soils retain water and do not permit further absorption. The ability of the soil to absorb water is called the percolation rate. If you dig below the topsoil and squeeze the soil into a ball in your hand, soil with a high percolation rate will crumble, even when wet. Any soil

Soil Percolation Test

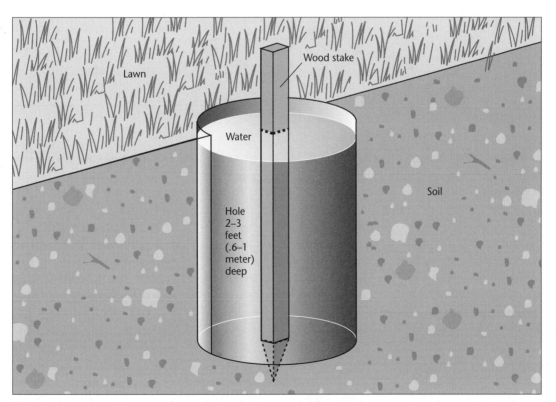

Fill hole with water and let set until water is absorbed; repeat. Refill hole with water and mark water level on the stake. Check in one hour; water level should drop at least 1 inch (2.5 centimeters).

Excavation/Retaining Wall

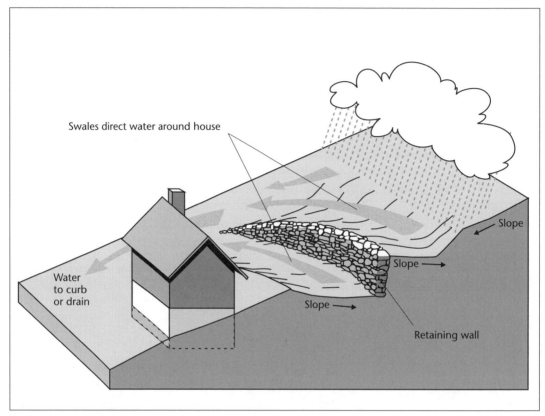

Swales direct water around house

Water to curb or drain

Slope

Slope

Slope

Retaining wall

One solution to drain a hilly lot. Swales—shallow trenches—direct water to storm sewers or drainage areas.

with a poor percolation rate—i.e., black or clay soil—will resemble a ball of Play Dough when squeezed in the hand.

To test the percolation rate of your soil, dig a hole that is 2 to 3 feet (0.6 to 1 meter) deep. Fill the hole with water and let the water percolate until the hole is empty. Repeat this procedure a second time. Then drive a wood stake, long enough to extend above the ground level, into the bottom of the hole. Again fill the hole with

water and mark the water level on the wood stake.

Let the water sit in the hole for one hour, then check the water level. If the water level has dropped 1 inch (2.5 centimeters) or more, you have good water absorption or percolation. If the water level has dropped very little, the soil will not absorb or hold much water, and the lawn will show water runoff during even a light to moderate rain.

If you cannot manage to control the water by absorp-

tion after taking the other steps recommended here, consider hiring a professional landscaper. He or she will either amend the soil by mixing it with peat moss or sand, or will remove it and replace it with soil that can absorb water more readily.

Perhaps one side of your lot slopes upward toward a hill, so that all the water that falls on the hill runs down toward your basement. You must manage that water runoff so that it is either held back or is diverted into slight

Excavation/Drain

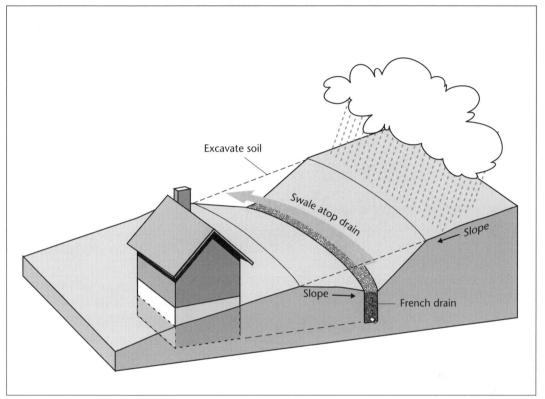

Excavate soil

Swale atop drain

Slope

Slope

French drain

To drain a hilly area, an alternate solution is to excavate the soil to create a slope away from the house, then build a French drain with swales to divert the water away from the house.

ditches or swales that are created at least 10 feet (3 meters) away from the basement.

To hold back the water runoff from a hill, you can build one or more terraces or retaining walls down the hillside. Build the retaining or terrace walls of stone or wood landscaping timbers. Be sure the terrace or retaining walls are built so there are drainage holes that allow the overflow water to flow through to the next level, and excess water cannot back up behind the walls.

Then, to ensure that the turf will absorb water, cultivate the soil behind the retaining walls and establish planting areas for flowers or shrubs. Do not cover the soil in these planting areas with plastic sheeting, because the goal is to have the water that flows into the area be absorbed into the soil, rather than being diverted to run down the hill toward the basement.

Landscaping features such as grass, flowers, shrubs, and trees will absorb

or retain a large amount of water. If you plant large shade trees be sure to keep them trimmed and the tops thinned out, so that sunlight can penetrate through the tree canopies to the lawn. After a rainfall, the sunlight will help evaporate excess water from the lawn.

Another technique is to divert water around the house via a slight depression called a swale. The swale is dug so that it is parallel to, and at least 10 feet (3 meters) from the basement wall,

French Drain

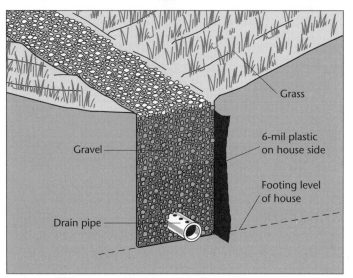

Grass

Gravel

6-mil plastic
on house side

Footing level
of house

Drain pipe

To build a French drain, dig a trench 2 feet (.6 meter) wide and deep
enough so the drain pipe is level with or below the house footing level.
Fill the trench with gravel or crushed rock.

Curtain Drain

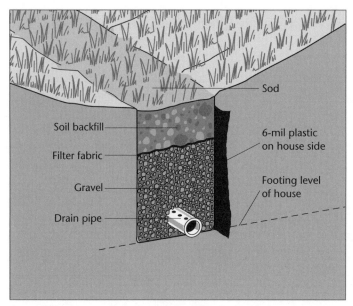

Sod

Soil backfill

Filter fabric

6-mil plastic
on house side

Gravel

Footing level
of house

Drain pipe

If you prefer grass to the gravel of a French drain, build a curtain drain.
Basic construction is the same, but a curtain drain is topped with soil and
sod. Note the depression or swale atop the drain.

then curves along the two sides of the house so water is diverted toward the street at the front of the house and into curbside gutters or storm drains. (See Swales illustration on page 30)

To build a proper swale, the lot first must be surveyed with a transit, the swale diversion area laid out, and the soil graded with a tractor. Care must be taken so that the swale does not divert the water onto a neighbor's lawn, thus creating a drainage problem on an adjacent lot. Swales are usually projects for landscape or excavating contractors. To find a contractor, look in the Yellow Pages under Excavating Contractors.

When the swale is completed the area should be covered with sod. Grass seed, tends to wash to the bottom of a slope before taking root.

STANDING WATER

During or immediately after a rain, check your lot for puddles or large areas of standing water. Use wood stakes, driven into the soil, to define the perimeter of puddles of standing water. Fill and level small puddle areas with a wheelbarrow of black dirt.

If you have large areas of standing water, consider having a contractor survey the area, then either fill the

Swales

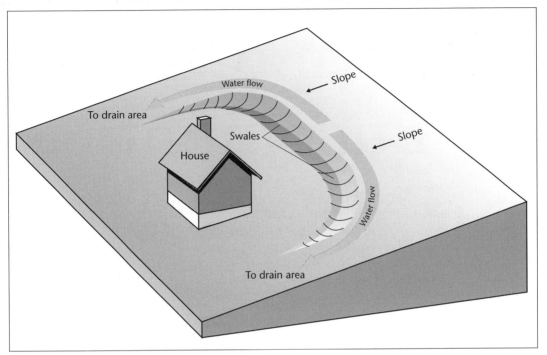

Swales are shallow trenches that direct water away from a house foundation to drainage areas. Call a landscape contractor for this project.

low areas with soil so water will not stand, or install perforated plastic drain pipes that will collect the water and divert it to the street or storm sewers. (See French Drain and Curtain Drain illustrations, opposite)

CHAPTER 3

Waterproofing an Existing/New Basement

The critical defenses in preventing a wet basement are installing a proper gutter system as discussed in Chapter 1, Wet Basements, and providing a proper grade on the lawn as discussed in Chapter 2, Correcting the Grade, thus preventing water from reaching the basement. Because water entry is pervasive, it is very difficult to effectively seal a basement against water entry if any substantial amount of water is allowed to reach the basement wall; water will penetrate the tiniest crack in the basement. Any concrete wall, whether poured concrete or block construction, will have some expansion cracks along its length, and will have a shrinkage crack where the basement wall meets the concrete slab floor. In addition to the cracks, concrete blocks are porous, and water will readily soak through the blocks under hydrostatic pressure. It is important to take every step possible to seal the basement against water entry, but remember that the basement wall itself is the last line of defense.

To prevent the potential damage of having water in the basement, take every step possible to block water entry (see chapters 1 and 2). The first is to try to stop the water entry, working from the exterior side of the basement.

Parging

A worker applies 50/50 sand and cement coat to seal and waterproof wall.

SEALING THE BASEMENT EXTERIOR

In chapters 1 and 2 we discussed the value of both gutters and a proper grade or slope to the lawn. In this chapter I'll discuss several other exterior projects to block water entry from the exterior of the basement.

First, check if window wells show any evidence of water entry. To provide good drainage and to help absorb any water that enters the window well, there should be a base layer of 2 to 4 inches (5 to 10 centimeters) of clean gravel at the bottom of the well. Reset and seal the window wells. Use concrete wall anchors to attach the plastic or metal window well securely against the concrete basement wall, so water cannot enter through any cracks between the window well and the wall. Use an acrylic latex exterior caulk to caulk these cracks.

Mortar Joints

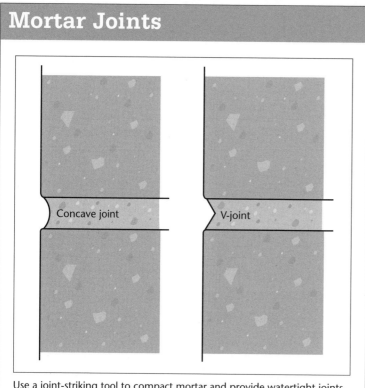

Use a joint-striking tool to compact mortar and provide watertight joints.

Finally, to ensure against water entry from falling rain or snow, buy and install plastic covers over all window wells. These clear plastic covers permit sunlight to enter the basement windows, but provide a barrier to entry of rain, snow, insects, animals, or dirt. With the help of the plastic well covers, basement window wells will stay clean and dry.

CAULKING

Another point of potential water entry is any crack where an exterior concrete slab, such as a walk, drive, or patio, is immediately adjacent to the basement wall. Remember that caulks

Caulking Cracks

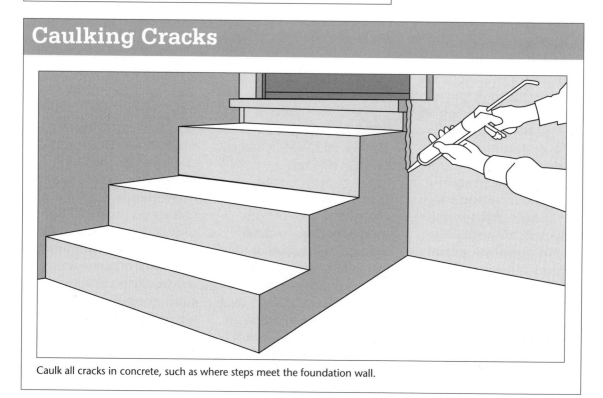

Caulk all cracks in concrete, such as where steps meet the foundation wall.

Exterior Sealer

A worker uses a roller or stiff broom to apply concrete mix to the foundation wall.

sealed, inspect the caulk seasonally to be sure there are no open cracks. In cold climates it is important to reseal any caulk before freezing temperatures and snow arrive in the fall, and before spring rains begin.

If the exterior of the concrete basement walls is unfinished, use a wire brush to clean away any buildup of dirt or efflorescence (see below), then use a product such as muriatic acid or UGL's DRYLOK Etch to thoroughly clean the concrete. Then apply two coats of waterproofing paints to the exposed concrete. Choose a paint that is formulated for use on masonry or concrete.

WATERPROOFING THE INTERIOR OF CONCRETE WALLS

After sealing the exterior side of basement walls against water entry, move next to the interior. The first step is to clean the concrete walls so the patchers and sealer will adhere properly. Always wear a dust mask when working on concrete.

Efflorescence is a white-to-gray powder that forms on a concrete surface when moisture activates salts within the concrete. The salts are found in the materials used to make the concrete, and may be sulfates of sodium, potassium, calcium, etc. In order for

usually are used to join two materials that have different expansion ratios and are subject to extreme ranges of temperature, so caulks often crack and must be resealed. In the past, when petroleum-based caulks were the only choice available, recaulking exterior cracks was an almost endless job because the petroleum caulks become brittle and crack with age. Modern caulks such as acrylic latex and silicone products remain elastic after curing, and will flex slightly as the caulked materials move or expand. Special caulks for patching both concrete and asphalt are available in caulking tubes. Ask your dealer to help you select the best caulk for your project.

Caulk any cracks between asphalt or concrete slabs and the basement wall. To prevent possible water entry, be sure the cracks are completely sealed. For filling large cracks, first pour clean sand or stuff fiberglass insulation into the crack to partially fill it, then seal with a caulk. After the crack is

Interior/Exterior Sealer

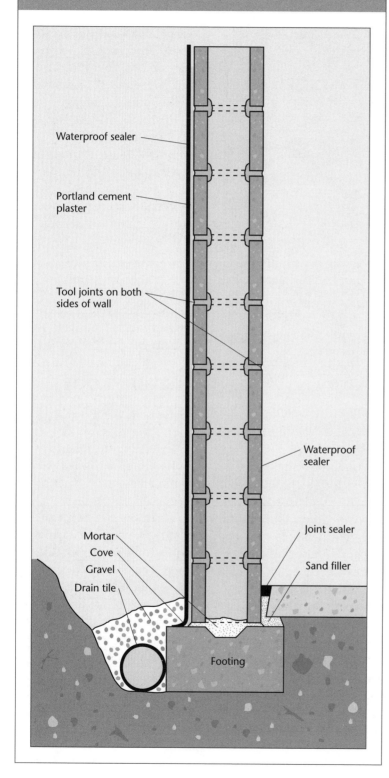

Waterproof sealer

Portland cement plaster

Tool joints on both sides of wall

Waterproof sealer

Mortar
Cove
Gravel
Drain tile

Joint sealer

Sand filler

Footing

efflorescence to appear on the surface of the concrete, there first must be salts present in the concrete, and there must be moisture to carry the salts to the surface through evaporation or hydrostatic pressure. To eliminate the surface buildup of efflorescence, take steps to prevent water from reaching the concrete wall, so there will be no moisture to cause leaching or move the efflorescence. Before applying a sealer to the walls, use a wire brush or grinding wheel to remove any heavy buildup of efflorescence. Clean the entire wall with a 5 percent solution of muriatic acid, or with a commercial concrete cleaner such as UGL's DRYLOK Etch. Wear rubber gloves and eye goggles when using acid or commercial cleaners.

Before starting to patch the basement walls, try to determine if the cracks are merely small expansion cracks, which are common because concrete expands and contracts with changes in the temperature, or are structural cracks that may indicate a serious problem with the structural integrity of the wall. If a crack runs from floor to ceiling, is more than ¼ inch (0.6 centimeter) wide, or if the edges of the crack have become misaligned, there may be a structural problem with the wall or its footings. If any

Water Control—Interior

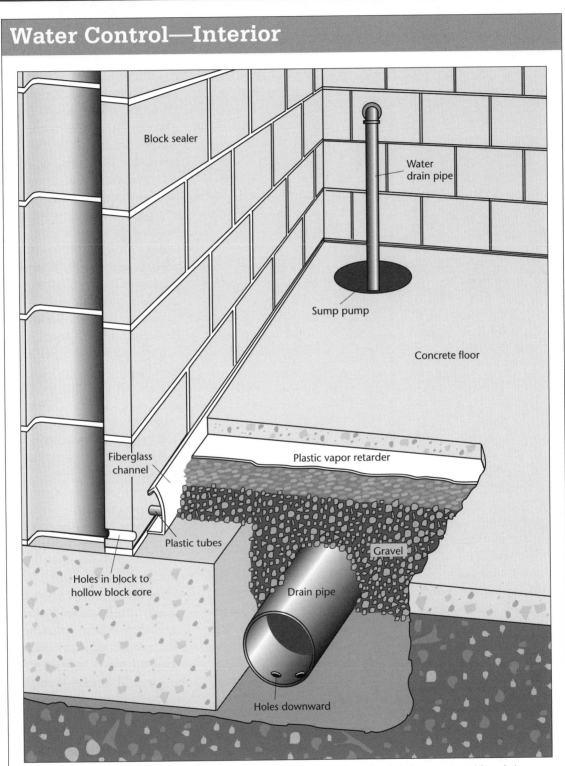

Block sealer

Water drain pipe

Sump pump

Concrete floor

Fiberglass channel

Plastic vapor retarder

Plastic tubes

Gravel

Holes in block to hollow block core

Drain pipe

Holes downward

Interior waterproofing includes baseboard drain tubes, block sealer, drain tubes into bottom row of foundation blocks, drain pipe, and a vapor retarder under the concrete floor slab.

such crack is present, have a masonry contractor inspect and appraise the condition of the wall before proceeding with waterproofing.

Next, clean any loose concrete or mortar from wall cracks. The major crack will usually occur between the concrete wall and the slab floor because the poured concrete slab contains a large volume of water, and the floor slab will shrink as the concrete cures and moisture leaves the slab.

A wide variety of concrete patch products is available at home centers. The patch product you select should be a hydraulic cement product such as DRYLOK Fast Plug. Hydraulic cement expands as it sets and can be applied even to cracks that are damp, or where water seepage is present in the crack.

Concrete patch products are available in a dry powder form, and are mixed either with plain water or with a catalyst liquid that is included with the box of patcher. Mix the crack patcher and apply it according to the manufacturer's instructions. Concrete patching products usually are quick-setting, but let the patched areas set for 24 hours before applying a concrete sealer to the walls.

To seal the concrete walls against water entry, choose one of the many available concrete sealers. One premium wall sealer is DRYLOK Waterproofer, containing Portland cement and synthetic rubber. These products come ready-mixed in 1-gallon (4 liter) pails, look much like white latex paint, and can be applied with brush, roller, or sprayer. To be sure the tiny holes in the concrete block are completely sealed, double-roll—i.e., roll the sealer in both directions—or scrub the sealer on with a fiber concrete brush. If you use spray equipment to apply the sealer, be sure to back-brush the sprayed sealer (i.e., brush the sealer out after applying it with the spray equipment). Back-brushing will ensure that tiny pores in the concrete are filled and sealed.

Concrete blocks have hollow cores, and any water that penetrates the blocks may accumulate in these cores. Because water that reaches the basement wall will flow down to the concrete footing level, then rise in the wall, the lower 2 to 3 feet (0.6 to 1 meter) of the wall is most prone to water entry. Because the water penetration usually is in the lower third of the wall, it is best to apply two coats of sealer to this area, with a single coat on the upper two-thirds of the wall.

To begin the sealer application, apply the sealer to the lower one-third of the wall, or whatever portion of the wall becomes visibly wet. Apply a generous coating of the material and work it well into the mortar joints, the corners, and the pores of the concrete. Allow this lower coat to dry as per the manufacturer's directions, usually for 24 hours, before applying a second coat of sealer.

Starting at the top of the wall, apply a second coat of sealer to the full wall, reapplying over the first coat on the lower portion. Again, to ensure a complete seal, it is important to work the sealer into any joints or pores in the concrete. Allow the sealer to dry. If the wall still has some water seepage, apply a third coat of sealer. When the wall shows no further seepage, follow with a coat of concrete finish paint if desired.

BASEMENT WATER-CONTROL PRODUCTS

The steps recommended to this point—gutters, proper grade or slope to the lawn, and a coat of waterproofing sealer—will eliminate the majority of wet basement problems. In rare instances, however, it may be impossible to eliminate water entry into the basement. For instance, if a patio or drive slab adjoins the basement wall and slopes toward the basement, the only remedy to keep water out is to remove and repave the concrete slab. If you want a less expensive solution, use a basement water control product, such as the Beaver Basement Water Control system. Keep in mind that the water entry may be through only one wall of the basement, so it is not necessary to install the system along all four basement walls. The wet wall alone will require application of the Beaver system.

The Beaver Basement Water Control system consists of a series of tubular plastic channels that are glued to the basement floor/wall juncture, much like baseboard trim. These must be glued to bare concrete blocks. The water flows into the channels via holes bored in each concrete block core in the bottom row of blocks. From the point of entry, the water flows through the channels to a floor drain or sump pump, which may pump the water through a disposal pipe to a remote spot on the lawn.

To install the Beaver system, drill holes from the basement interior into the hollow core of each individual bottom concrete block. Then insert plastic tubing into each hole. Next, using an adhesive supplied with the system, glue the tubular channels to the concrete floor. The plastic water tubes from the block cores are inserted into the back side of the plastic tubular channels. The tubular channels are adhesively attached to one another, and 90-degree corner connectors permit you to turn the channels around corners if necessary. The tubular channels terminate at the floor drain or sump pump.

Other types of water control products are also available. Many of these plastic drain channels require that you break out a trench in the perimeter of the concrete floor, install plastic tubing to connect the hollow block cores to the channels, then install a sump pump to remove any entry water. Because it is installed against the wall, and you avoid the work and expense of breaking up the concrete floor and then patching the slab, the Beaver system mentioned above is a much cleaner and cheaper installation than those that require breakup of concrete.

WATERPROOFING A NEW BASEMENT

When having a new house or a room addition built, be sure the masonry contractor follows the necessary procedures for ensuring a dry basement. These steps depend upon your region and soil type, which can vary widely over a distance of only a mile or less (¾ kilometer). If you check the soil that has been removed during basement excavations at nearby building sites, you may find that at one site the soil is very sandy, while a short distance away the excavated soil will be heavy black or clay soil. The precautions needed to ensure a dry basement may be expensive, but it is best to err on the side of caution to ensure a trouble-free basement.

To ensure that your new basement will be dry, check the building code for the requirements in your area, and check personally as the work progresses to be sure the builder has met those code requirements. Insist on inspecting the open excavation before it is backfilled with dirt, while you can see any drain pipes or waterproof coatings. One idea is to photograph the pipes before they are covered, in case of future problems.

WATERPROOFING CONCRETE WALLS

The first barrier to water entry through a concrete wall is the type of concrete block and mortar used, and the way the wall is constructed. The poured concrete or concrete blocks must be made with a high cement content, properly graded aggregates, and a low water/cement ratio.

Air-entrained concrete is concrete that is mixed with additives that improve resistance to freezing and is more watertight because it is more dense than concrete that is not entrained. If you are building a new basement, ask the contractor to use the best quality concrete blocks or mix.

To resist water entry, the mortar joints between the blocks should be no more than ⅜ inch (.7 centimeter) wide. Some masons strike or rake the joints, a process that refers to the use of a sharp tool to simply scrape the excess mortar out of the joint. This leaves a mortar joint that may have voids or burrs that can hold water. The best technique is to use a concave or V-shaped tool to smooth or tool the joints so the mortar is tightly compressed and smoothed on the mortar surface. This approach will help ensure watertight mortar joints between the blocks. (See "Mortar Joints" illustration on page 36.)

After the block walls are laid up, the exterior sides of the walls should be plastered with two ¼-inch (0.5-centimeter) thick coats of mortar. This process is called "parging" the walls. The plaster used should be a 1:1 mortar mix, or one part of Portland cement mixed with one part of fine sand. To ensure good bonding

between the plaster or parge coat and the block wall, the concrete wall should be slightly dampened before the first coat of plaster is applied. The coating is troweled to form a cove at the footing level to shed water at the joint between the footing and the block wall. The first plaster coat should extend from the footing level up to a point 6 inches (15 centimeters) above the finished grade. To ensure adhesion of the second coat, the surface of the first plaster coat is roughened or scarified while still wet. After the first coat has cured, it is wetted so the second plaster coat will adhere to it.

If the basement is being built in heavy black or clay soils, as extra insurance against water entry, two coats of a bituminous waterproof coating should be brushed on after the exteriors of the walls are plastered with the mortar mix.

In very severe cases an alternative approach is to apply a waterproof membrane over the bituminous coating. The membrane is used to cover the exterior of the wall, from the bottom of the concrete footings to the finished grade. (See "Exterior Sealer" illustration on page 37.)

WATERPROOFING THE BASEMENT FLOOR

Because of capillary action, water from the soil can wick up and penetrate the basement floor slab. In addition to having the contractor waterproof the basement walls, insist on having a vapor barrier laid on the earth or fill before the basement floor is poured. The vapor barrier may be 6-mil polyethylene plastic sheeting, two-ply hot-mopped felts, or 55-pound (25-kilogram) rolled roofing. (Sand is spread over the vapor barrier so it will not be punctured during concrete placement.) Whichever material is selected, the material should be carefully installed, overlapped at least 6 inches (15 centimeters), and sealed at all seams.

PERIMETER DRAIN TILES

As a final barrier to basement water entry, install drain pipes around the exterior perimeter of the concrete footings. These drain pipes are usually plastic and are perforated by small holes on the top. The perforations permit any water that reaches the footings to flow into the drain pipes, which are installed at a slight slope so collected water can flow by gravity to a sump area or to a storm sewer drain.

To install the drain pipes, workers will first place 2 to 4 inches (5 to 10 centimeters) of gravel in the trench as a bed for the pipes to rest upon. Then they install the drain pipes so the bottom of the pipes are level with the bottom of the concrete footings. To prevent soil or silt from seeping into the pipes and clogging them, tar paper is placed over the joints where pipe ends meet. Next, a 12-inch (30-centimeter) layer of washed gravel is placed over the drain pipes. When the gravel is in place, the contractor will use a tractor to backfill the excavation, or to push the soil in place against the basement wall.

In severe cases where there is a high water table, drain pipes are installed on both the outside and inside perimeters of the basement. To avoid an endless battle with water problems, a better choice might be to build a half-basement that extends only 4 feet (1.25 meters) into the ground, such as those seen in a split-level house, or build over a crawl space or a slab on grade.

PART II

THE REST OF THE HOUSE

CHAPTER 4

Roof Leaks

Because it covers and protects all other components from the elements, the roof may be the most important part of a house. Inspect the roof for signs of age and damage each spring before windstorms and rains begin, and again each fall before winter's onslaught. Also check the home interior—the attic, ceilings, and walls—for any sign of water entry or damage. With periodic inspection you can catch roof leaks quickly, minimizing the extent of the damage and repair costs.

SHINGLE CONSTRUCTION

Because the majority of roofs in North America are covered with asphalt shingles, I've directed my advice to those readers with asphalt shingles.

If you can determine the age and construction of the shingles, you will be able to determine how much longer they will last. Until 20 years ago, asphalt shingles had a felt or tar paper base and an asphalt coating. To help protect the shingles from solar damage, the asphalt coating was covered with gravel. The warranty for these older shingles varies widely: the thicker and heavier the shingles, the longer the warranty. Depending on the quality and weight of the shingles the old-style shingle carried a warranty of between 15 and 20 years.

However, the life of shingles also depends on other

Roof Waterproofing

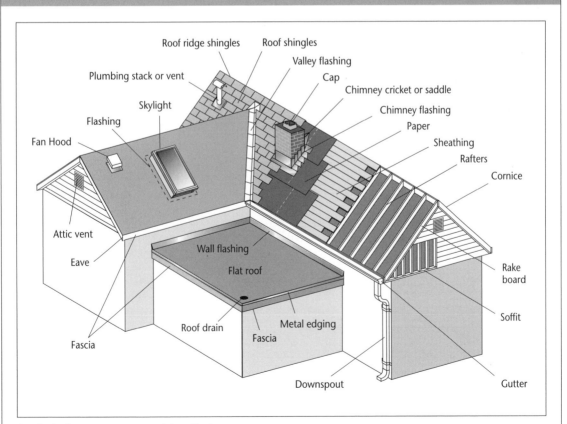

Roof ridge shingles
Roof shingles
Valley flashing
Plumbing stack or vent
Cap
Chimney cricket or saddle
Skylight
Chimney flashing
Flashing
Paper
Fan Hood
Sheathing
Rafters
Cornice
Attic vent
Wall flashing
Eave
Flat roof
Rake board
Roof drain
Metal edging
Fascia
Soffit
Fascia
Downspout
Gutter

Any flashed area poses a potential roof leak.

factors, including the severity of the weather in the area in which you live. High summertime temperatures will dry out the shingles, making them brittle and subject to cracking. Frequent windstorms can also flex the shingles and cause them to crack or break. Severe hailstorms damage or weaken shingles. Although the hail may not penetrate through the shingles to cause immediate leaks, the repeated battering of the hail will shorten the life of the shingles.

Modern shingles (made in the last 20 years) have a durable fiberglass mat base, and ceramic granules rather than gravel finish. They also have self-sealing tabs. These are strips of adhesive on the shingle lower tabs that soften from the heat of the sun and glue the tabs down so they will not become windblown. All nails are driven through the upper edge where they are covered by next row of shingles. For several years fiberglass shingles have been offered with warranties of 25 or even 35 years.

FINDING ROOF LEAKS

When a wet spot appears on a ceiling, many homeowners assume that the leak in the roof is directly above the wet ceiling. Often that is not the case. Water may leak through a roof and run down along a roof rafter until the water meets a knot or splinter on the bottom side of the rafter. The flaw in the rafter causes an interruption of the water's path, and that is where the water will drip off the rafter onto the ceiling below. For this rea-

Valley Flashing

Upper flashing pieces overlap the lower flashing

Proper roof flashing techniques prevent leaks.

son, it may be difficult to locate and patch a leak in the roof.

If you have a stain or a wet spot on a ceiling, use a flashlight with a bright beam to check the attic. First, pull back any ceiling insulation over the wet spot and inspect the water damage. If the area is simply damp, leave the insulation pulled back from the wet spot so air can reach and dry it. When the ceiling and insulation are completely dry, replace the insulation between the rafters.

Standing water on a ceiling surface will result in serious and extensive damage to the wallboard or plaster, so you should act quickly to remove the standing water. If there is standing water on the attic side of the ceiling, place a pail under the spot to catch the water, then bore a hole through the wallboard or plaster ceiling to let the water drain through and escape. Ceilings that are wetted only for a short period will usually be easy to repair.

Because water is present and there is danger of a shock from using an electric drill, use a hand drill or a cordless battery-powered drill to make the drain hole through the ceiling. A drill bit that is ¼ inch (0.5 centimeter) in diameter will usually make a hole large enough to allow the water to

Finding the Leak

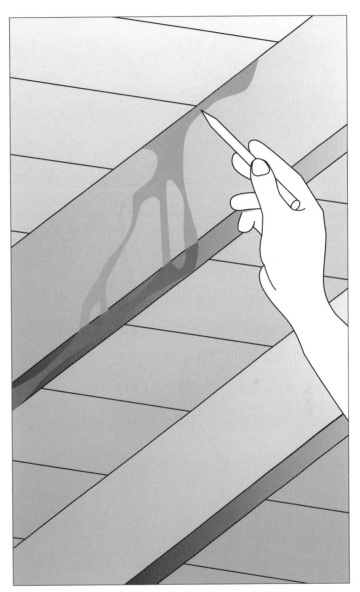

Look for water stains on the roof sheathing to find a leak.

drain through. When all standing water has drained, leave the insulation pulled away from the area until the ceiling and insulation are dry. You can speed the drying process by placing a

small fan, directed at the repair area, in the attic. If the leak is near an electric ceiling fixture, turn off the circuit and have an electrician clean and dry the fixture.

When the area is dry,

Bore a Drain Hole in Ceiling

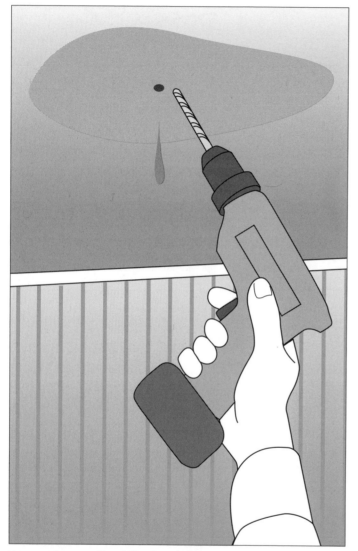

Use an awl or a cordless drill to bore a drain hole in the ceiling to let water run out.

Then sand lightly, apply a coat of sealer over the patch area, and repaint.

To find the leak, use your flashlight and inspect the underside of the roof sheathing and the rafters near the leak for stains or wetness. Do this during or immediately after a rain. Often you can see and trace the rain's entry path. While in the attic, calculate the location so that you can find the exact location from the exterior of the roof. For example, if the water entry is near a furnace stack, roof vent, valley, or fireplace chimney, you can climb onto the roof and use the chimney or stack as a reference point to find the leak area and make a permanent repair.

If you cannot locate the leak from inside the attic, inspect the roof carefully. The most common points for roof water entry are along valleys, or at chimney or furnace stack flashings. Check around the flashing to find the point of water entry. Inspect the flashing for any holes or rusted areas, and use a fiberglass repair kit to patch them. Often, liberal application of roof mastic along the top and sides of the flashing will stop the leak. If these steps are unsuccessful in patching the leak, or there are signs of extensive problems, call in a professional roofer.

patch the hole you have drilled in the ceiling by using a taping knife to spread premixed taping compound over the repair area. Then embed a piece of fiber wallboard tape over the hole. Use the knife to smooth the patch and to remove excess taping compound. When the tape is dry, apply a second coat of compound over the patch, smoothing the edges of the patch with the knife. Apply a third coat if necessary to conceal the tape.

Roof Leak

Place a pail in the attic to catch water from leak.

ROOF ICE DAMS

In cold winter climates, roof ice dams can cause roof leaks. Although most ice dam problems occur in the north, ice dams may be a problem as far south as Texas.

If you get a snow buildup on your roof, and the weather warms up, the sun will quickly remove the snow by melting it from the top down, and no ice dam will form. The conditions that produce roof ice dams develop when both snowfall and an extended period of cold weather occur. Then the snow lingers on the roof. As heat escapes from the house interior, upward through the ceilings, there is a heat buildup in the attic, with the warmest temperatures being at the highest point or ridge of the attic. This warm air will melt the snow on the highest points of the roof. The water will run down the roof, under the remaining snow, to the eaves. At the eave level the attic temperatures are cooler, so the water may freeze there or at the soffits to form a dam that will trap the water. The water will continue to melt at the higher levels of the roof, run down to the ice dam, and form a pool of water. The ice dam causes the water to back up and run under the shingles. Water entry due to ice dams will usually cause a stain or wet area at or near the point where the ceiling meets the outside walls. (See "Ice Dam" illustration on page 52.)

The most effective way to eliminate ice dams is to correct the ceiling insulation and attic ventilation to eliminate heat buildup in the attic, i.e., establish a cold roof deck. First check the recommended ceiling insulation depths, or R-factor, for your area. Then measure the ceiling insulation depth to be sure your insulation meets current recommendations. If it does not, have additional insulation blown into the ceiling. Be sure that the insulation layer extends past the top wall plates—i.e., the horizontal top 2 ×4 or 2 × 6 of the wall—but does not completely block ventilation from the soffit area into the attic. Back

Ice Dam

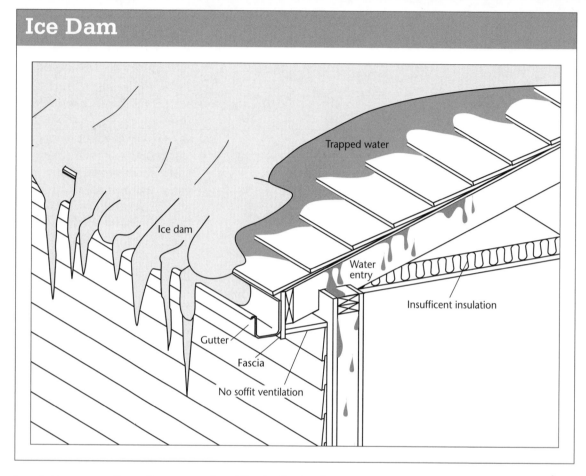

Trapped water

Ice dam

Water entry

Insufficent insulation

Gutter

Fascia

No soffit ventilation

insulation away from the soffits just enough to permit air to flow from soffit to attic. Also inspect the attic area for heat leaks—voids or cracks where heat can pass through the ceiling and enter the attic. These heat leaks often occur around ceiling light outlets, where furnace stacks or plumbing vents penetrate the ceiling, or around attic access doors. To seal the heat leak areas, fill even the smallest void or crack with fiberglass insulation. Caution: do not cover the attic side of recessed light fixtures with insula-

tion. The bulbs in the recessed lights generate a lot of heat, and insulation atop the fixture may cause a fire.

When insulation levels are up to code, check the attic ventilation. The best attic ventilation is continuous soffit/ridge vent. This means that vents are uninterrupted from end to end of the house, as opposed to the installation of individual vents at selected points along the soffits and ridge or roof deck. Newer houses usually have continuous soffit/ridge venting, but houses built more than ten years

ago may have inadequate attic ventilation. If your attic ventilation is substandard and you are planning on re-roofing soon, be sure to have the continuous soffit/ridge vents installed as part of the roofing project. Wait until you reroof , using existing vents. Roof vents remove hot air and moisture. If you have ice dams, ask a contractor to install more vents—select type from the illustrations.

The theory of having continuous soffit/ridge venting is based on the fact that warm air rises, a phenome-

Attic Ventilation

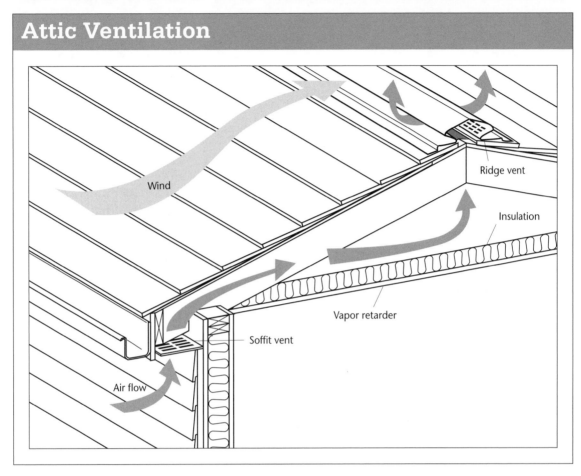

non called the chimney effect. As attic air is warmed, it rises and exits through the ridge vents. As the warm air moves out through the higher ridge vents, cooler air is pulled into the attic through the soffit vents, moves across the insulation to remove any moisture in the attic, is warmed, and rises to exit at the ridge vents. This process does not depend on power fans or ventilators, but is a natural process caused by the hot air rising.

With adequate ceiling and proper ventilation, the temperature in the attic will not vary widely from ridge to soffit levels. Snow will then be melted from the top side by the sun and run off the roof, rather than forming ice dams at the eaves.

Some homeowners cover attic vents in winter, hoping to save on heating costs. But once heat has escaped into the attic, it is no longer heating the house, and should be exhausted to prevent ice dams.

There is currently some argument between experts on the value of attic ventilation in preventing ice dams. Nevertheless, it seems reasonable to assume that, no matter the depth of insulation, some heat will escape into the attic. Unless that heat, and any additional heat generated from the sun, is vented outside, it will melt the snow from the bottom or shingle side, even on cold and sunless days, and ice dams will form at the cold soffits. (Heat rises and melts the snow at the upper roof or ridge; the lower roof to the soffits stays cold so water refreezes at the soffits.) Proper attic ventilation is absolutely

Continuous Soffit Vent

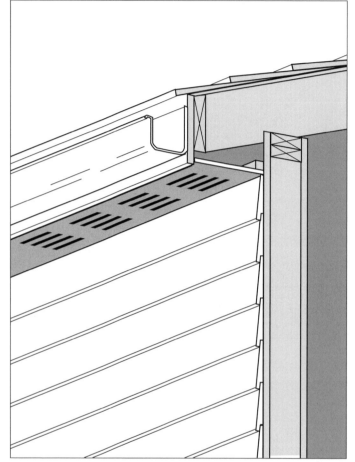

Soffit vent in trim provides provides ventilation along the length of the soffit.

retain water but will also block the drainage slots, called keyways, between the shingles. The resulting moisture buildup will support the growth of mildew or moss.

If mildew (fungus) or moss (plant) are already present on your roof, ask your home center to recommend a fungicide or herbicide product to kill the growth. If you do not wish to do the treatment yourself, hire a roofer to perform the task.

INSPECTING A ROOF

It is essential to perform a roof inspection while standing on the roof, where you can have a close-up view of the ridge, valleys, flashing, and shingles. If your roof is too high or steep to climb, or you are physically unable to climb, have a professional roofer do the inspection.

Check the appearance and condition of the shingles. Signs of shingle failure include uneven or curling shingle tabs; a ragged edge at the tabs, which indicates wear and weathering; missing or broken shingles; and excessive loss of granules.

As the shingles age and dry out from solar exposure, the surface granules will loosen and be washed by rain down the roof deck. Check in the gutters and at splash blocks under

essential to eliminate ice dams.

CLEANING THE ROOF

If you have a roof covered with wood shingles or shakes, you may have problems with mildew or moss growing on the wood surfaces. In order for either to grow, moisture must be

present. Often the moisture will be retained on the shingles because of shade trees whose canopies overhang the roof deck. Hire a tree trimmer to thin the crown of the trees, so that sunlight and wind can penetrate to dry the roof deck.

Clean the roof deck often to remove any twigs, leaves, or other debris. This debris not only will

Continuous Ridge Vent

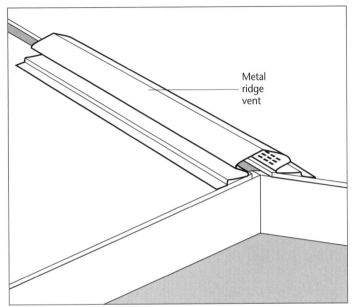

Metal ridge vent

A 1-½-inch (3.8 centimeter) gap in the sheathing at the ridge is covered by this metal ridge vent, which provides ventilation for the entire attic.

ground pipes for a buildup of granules.

Next, check the ridge row. These are the shingles that cover the ridge or peak of the roof where two ascending slopes rise and meet. Replace or repair missing or damaged ridge shingles.

A valley is the point on the roof where two shingled areas or descending planes meet. Check the shingles near the valleys and the flashing of the valley. On a minority of roofs the shingles will be woven together at the valleys, but metal or fiberglass flashing is the common valley treatment. Any interruption in the roof shingles—valleys,

Gable Vents

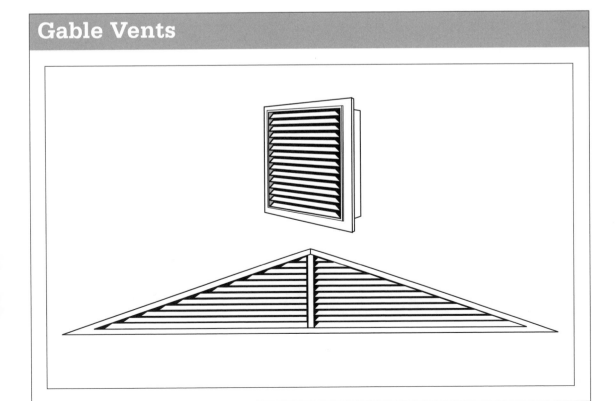

Power Vent

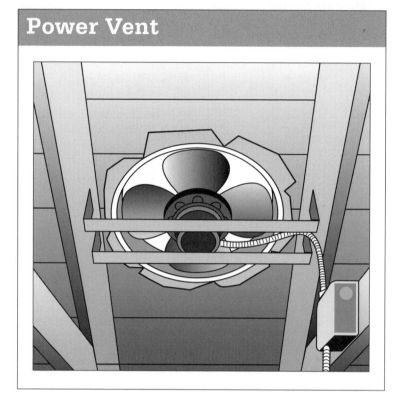

Valley Flashing

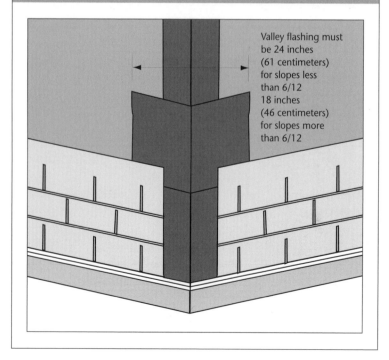

Valley flashing must be 24 inches (61 centimeters) for slopes less than 6/12 18 inches (46 centimeters) for slopes more than 6/12

flashing, vents—is a possible source of leaks.

On roofs more than 20 years old, galvanized steel flashing was used. Unfortunately, galvanized flashing eventually, loses its zinc coating, and the steel will rust, depending on the quality of the material. If you discover your flashing has lost its coating, but rust is not yet evident, paint the flashing with a paint formulated for metal application, such as Galva-Grip or Rustoleum. If the galvanized valleys are already rusting, use sandpaper or a wire brush to remove as much rust as possible, then paint the flashings using one of the recommended paint products.

For the past 20 years prefinished aluminum flashing is more commonly used. Aluminum is the preferred metal because it does not rust and needs no maintenance. Inspect aluminum flashing for storm damage such as dents or holes, and reflash where necessary.

In addition to valley flashing, metal flashings are used between shingles and siding where the roof changes plane or direction, such as where the roof of a garage or addition does not match the level of the house roof and forms a juncture with the wall siding.

Inspect the flashing around any interruptions in

Roof Leak

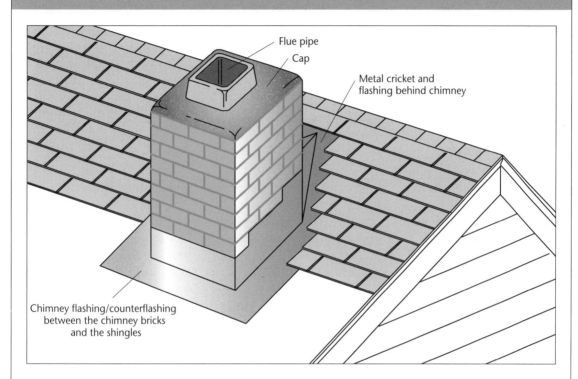

Flue pipe
Cap
Metal cricket and flashing behind chimney
Chimney flashing/counterflashing between the chimney bricks and the shingles

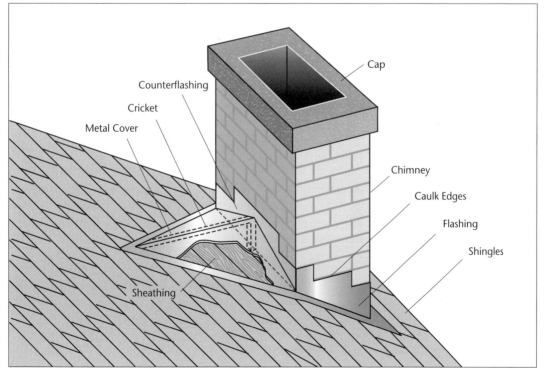

Counterflashing
Cricket
Metal Cover
Sheathing
Cap
Chimney
Caulk Edges
Flashing
Shingles

the roof deck, such as flashings used where a furnace stack, plumbing vent, or fireplace chimney penetrate the roof. Be sure the flashings are intact and are securely fastened to the roof. If there is a problem with water entry where the high side of the roof meets a fireplace chimney, have a roofer install a metal device, called a cricket, to divert the water around the chimney. (See "Roof Leak" illustration on page 57.)

If the shingles are not sealed against the flashing, use roof mastic to caulk the cracks between the shingles and the flashing. The roof mastic may become brittle and crack with age, so make annual or even seasonal inspections of the mastic and renew as necessary.

TIME TO RE-ROOF

If the roof is more than 15 years old, if it exhibits any of the aging symptoms mentioned above (see Inspecting a Roof, page 54) or if there is a problem with roof leaks that do not respond to repair efforts, it may be time to re-roof. Most building codes permit a re-roof directly over a roof that has only one layer of shingles; for good building practice, if the roof has two layers of shingles you must have all shingles and flashing removed down to the roof deck or sheathing and start anew.

As already mentioned, the roof may be the most important component of the house, because it covers and protects all other components. Although re-roofing is an expensive project, the damage that can result from water entry can far exceed the cost of a roof, so having a sound roof is good insurance to protect the entire structure.

Although shingles are widely available from home centers, shingle manufacturers once ignored the D-I-Y business. Roofing is hard and heavy work; it is performed at dangerous heights; it requires use of scaffold that must be rented; and a high skill level is necessary to achieve a weathertight roof. For example, few homeowners could successfully flash the point where a garage-level roof meets the house siding, or where the shingles meet a masonry chimney, or install a cricket to divert water around a chimney. You also must dispose of the old roof material. For all these reasons, it is best to have a new roof installed by professionals.

To find a professional roofer, contact the local office of the National Association of Home Builders (NAHB), or the National Association for the Remodeling Industry (NARI). In Canada, check your local Association of Home Builders, or check NAHB.org on the Internet. These are associations that were formed by contractors to provide honest and professional service to the public. They each have codes of conduct and are self-policing.

Choose the materials wisely. Remember that the labor costs are equal regardless of the quality of the shingles. If you select a quality shingle with an extended warranty of 35 years, you can ensure that you won't need another roof for a long time.

CHAPTER 5

Vapor Retarders/Air Barriers

Whether liquid or vapor, water in any form will seek its own level, and will travel through any avenue available to reach equalization. In a building this phenomenon is called vapor pressure, and it can have serious implications for your house. The amount of moisture contained in the air varies with the air temperature; warm air can hold more moisture than cold air. This is the reason that meteorologists refer to the "relative humidity"—that is, the amount of moisture that is contained in the air relative to the amount of moisture it could contain at a given temperature.

As seasons change and outdoor air becomes colder, the relative humidity of that air drops. At that point, the warmer air inside the house will hold more moisture than the outside air. Because of this difference in vapor pressure, the moisture will attempt to migrate through the wall and equalize with the dry outdoor air. This process, the migration of water vapor through materials, is called diffusion.

As the warm, moisture-laden air passes through the wall or ceiling, it may meet a cooler surface within the framing structure. The water vapor will then condense and form water droplets on the material at that point. The point in the wall at which water vapor condenses is called the dew point. This moisture migration through the walls and ceilings of the house can produce wet and ineffective insulation, wood rot, mold

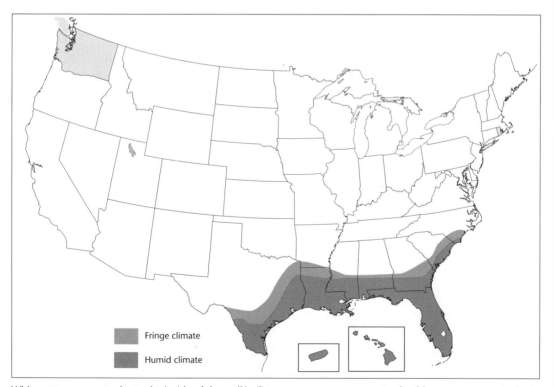

Vapor Retarder Requirements: U.S., By Region

Fringe climate

Humid climate

White area: vapor retarder to the inside of the wall/ceiling; grey area, no vapor retarder; blue area, vapor retarder to the exterior side of the wall/ceiling; ie, under exterior siding.

Building Material R-Factors

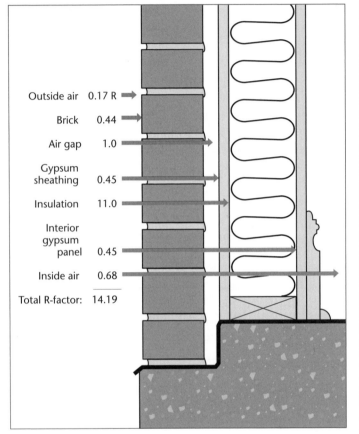

Outside air	0.17 R
Brick	0.44
Air gap	1.0
Gypsum sheathing	0.45
Insulation	11.0
Interior gypsum panel	0.45
Inside air	0.68
Total R-factor:	14.19

Insulation or R-factors of materials in exterior walls for brick veneer construction.

installed vapor or air barrier will greatly reduce the flow of moisture vapor and air from outside to inside, or vice versa.

Usually a 4-mil polyethylene film is installed on the warm side of the wall to serve as both a vapor retarder and an air barrier. Materials commonly installed between the sheathing and the exterior siding, such as 15-pound (7 kilogram) felt, Tyvek Housewrap, and paper-backed metal lath, are true vapor/air barriers.

In houses that are more than 30 years old there usually is no effective vapor retarder in either walls or ceilings. This lack of a vapor retarder caused fewer problems in older houses because there was no insulation in the wall cavities—the space between studs or joists—to trap moisture. The moisture passed through until it met the only barrier in the wall: the exterior paint. The most common moisture complaint in older houses is peeling exterior paint. If you own one of these older houses, to provide a vapor barrier you can apply a coat of alkyd (oil) sealer or paint on the interior surface of exterior walls and ceilings. Then prepare and repaint the exterior siding with an acrylic latex paint. This latex paint breathes,

or mildew, condensation and peeling paint on the house exterior. Vapor retarders/air barriers are intended to retard or bar the passage or diffusion of moisture or air through the walls or ceilings of a house.

The rate at which moisture penetrates or permeates material is a unit of measure called a "perm." Technically speaking, one perm is one drop of water per square foot (0.1 meter) per hour, per unit of vapor pressure difference. A vapor retarder is a material that has a resistance to diffusion of one perm or less of water vapor.

Vapor retarders were once called vapor barriers, but the term was a misnomer because most materials will permit some vapor passage through the walls or ceiling and thus will not completely bar vapor or moisture passage but simply retard or slow it. A properly

No Vapor Retarder

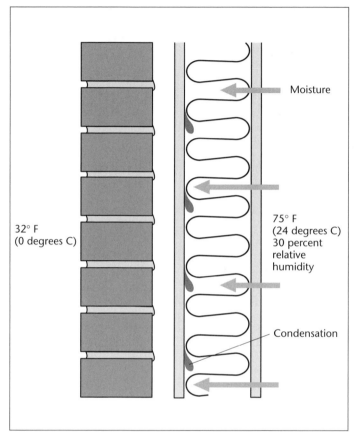

32° F
(0 degrees C)

75° F
(24 degrees C)
30 percent
relative
humidity

Moisture

Condensation

Brick veneer construction without vapor retarder. Moisture passes through the wall until it reaches exterior siding, condenses into liquid.

or permits moisture to pass through the paint coat rather than peeling the paint.

Early types of batt insulation, common in the '60s, sometimes had a face layer of kraft paper or aluminum foil that was intended to serve as a vapor retarder, but most of that insulation was improperly or sloppily installed. For example, both kraft and aluminum foil-faced insulation batts had edge tabs that were intended to be folded together over the face of the framing stud or joist, and stapled tightly to those faces. However, most of that batt insulation was simply stapled to the sides of the joist, leaving open seams between the kraft paper or aluminum facing and the framing. Large holes were cut around electrical outlet boxes; therefore, the faced insulation contained many voids and

did not provide a continuous vapor retarder.

Water vapor or air will pass through even a slight gap. For example, United States Gypsum, a major manufacturer whose wallboard trade name is Sheetrock™, estimates that assuming an interior/exterior pressure differential equal to a 9.3 mph (15 kph) wind, 31 *pounds* (14 kg) of water could pass in one month through a 1-inch square (2.5 centimeter) gap around an electrical outlet. If you multiply that amount of water by the number of outlets and other leaks in a house, you will see that we are attempting to deal with a serious moisture problem.

The second way in which water vapor can pass into a wall or ceiling is by air leakage, called convection. Because moisture and air can pass through a tiny void, extreme care must be taken when installing the vapor retarder. To provide a continuous shield, all sheets of polyethylene must be overlapped and the seams sealed with tape or acoustic sealant. Also, use tape or sealant to seal joints at any opening cut in the film, such as at windows, doors, electrical outlets, or heating ducts. Workers, especially drywall workers, electricians, and plumbers, must take care to avoid damaging the plastic while installing other finish materials.

Retarder Voids

75° F
(24 degrees C)
30 percent
relative
humidity

Electrical outlet

Air leakage

Condensation

If vapor retarder is not sealed at electrical outlets, windows, etc., air passes into wall cavity and condenses on colder brick veneer.

can result in thousands of dollars in damage to the bathroom and tile.

VAPOR RETARDERS IN CEILINGS

Until the oil embargo in the '70s it was common practice to install a vapor retarder only in the walls. The theory was that wall vapor retarders would prevent moisture from migrating through the walls, wetting insulation, peeling exterior paint, and damaging building components. But moisture was allowed to pass by diffusion through the ceilings and into the attic, where it could be exhausted through roof/attic vents. In those days, when we were assured by utility companies that we had a plentiful supply of cheap energy, only 4 inches (10 centimeters) of fiberglass insulation was standard in ceilings, even in the coldest climates. Thus there was little concern that the escaping moisture might be trapped in the thin insulation blanket.

In an effort to promote energy conservation, building codes then were changed to require a vapor retarder in ceilings and walls as well as thicker attic insulation blankets that would trap the escaping moisture. Because water is a good thermal conductor, wet insulation will

VAPOR RETARDERS IN BATHROOMS

It is important never to install two vapor retarders in the same wall, because moisture may become trapped between the two retarders and cause extensive moisture damage. For this reason, never install a vapor retarder in a bathroom tub/shower area that will be covered by ceramic tile. The tile itself is a vapor retarder, and installing polyethylene film beneath the tile substrate may result in moisture becoming trapped between the tile and the vapor retarder, with possible deterioration of the tile substrate and failure of the tile job. *This is an important point: many how-to texts show illustrations in which a tile substrate is applied over a polyethylene vapor retarder. This is a serious technical error, and* warm your house no better than wet socks will warm your feet. In climates where there are four distinct seasons, houses built since 1980 have ceiling vapor retarders.

If you live in an area where there are freezing temperatures in winter, it is easy to check the effectiveness of both the ceiling vapor retarder and attic ventilation. Go into the attic on a subfreezing day and check trusses, framing, and the underside of the roof plywood sheathing. Even in the best conditions you may see a very light layer of frost on the attic framing. If there is a moisture buildup in the attic you will see a substantial layer of frost on some or all of these components. If there is visible frost in only limited areas, suspect that there is a void in the vapor retarder at those locations. Inspect the area below the frost buildup for any leaks or voids in the vapor retarder, and seal those voids with tape or a sealant.

The code change requiring full vapor retarders has improved the energy or thermal efficiency of houses, but has created new problems. If the retarders are properly installed they can create the effect of living inside a plastic bag. Any moisture that enters the house interior cannot escape by diffusion or convection, and the moisture generated by daily family activities can build up to objectionable or even damaging and unhealthy levels.

One way to defeat high humidity in a tightly built home is to install an air-to-air heat exchanger. This is a device that has a duct that exhausts warm, moist air outdoors and a duct for dry incoming air. The ducts meet in an exchanger where the heat from the exhaust air is passed on to warm the incoming air, so that moisture is exhausted, but the heat in the air is reclaimed. If your contractor advises it, it is wise to install an air-to-air heat exchanger at the time of new construction, or to add one as a retrofit in a house that has problems with moisture. For a further discussion of indoor humidity problems, see Chapter 6, Humidity Problems.

INSTALLING A VAPOR RETARDER IN AN EXISTING CEILING

To check whether your house has a ceiling vapor retarder, go into the attic and pull back the ceiling insulation. If you have no vapor retarder in your ceiling, many texts suggest that you remove the insulation and install strips of poly plastic between the ceiling joists, then replace the insulation. However, as mentioned above, moisture and air will leak through the tiniest hole, rendering the vapor retarder ineffective. Sealing the seams between the plastic vapor retarder strips and the ceiling joists will be difficult. There will be no continuous retarder because the plastic will not cover the wood joists, and there will be two seams to seal between every joist cavity.

If you decide to install a vapor retarder in an existing ceiling, cut the poly strips so they are 6 inches (9 centimeters) wider than the space between each joist. Remove the insulation between the joists and center the plastic strip in the cavity, so the edges fold up about 3 inches (7.5 centimeters) onto each joist. Now use an acoustical sealant to seal the plastic retarder to the joists on either side of the cavity. Carefully replace the insulation between the joists.

A simpler solution, and one that is much easier than working in an attic, would be to remove any ceiling light fixtures, and seal any gap between the wallboard or plaster and the light box with an acoustical sealant. This will reduce air convection and moisture flow through these openings. Then apply a coat of alkyd sealer to all the ceilings in the house. This will act as a vapor retarder from the finished side of the ceiling.

Repaint or spray texture the ceilings as desired.

VAPOR RETARDERS IN WARM CLIMATES

Conventional advice is to install the vapor retarder on the inside of the wall, between the wallboard and the studs. But in warm, humid climates, the outdoor moisture levels may be higher than indoor moisture levels, so the pressure for movement of water vapor may be from the exterior to the interior. Such a warm, humid climate is found in the southeastern coastal area of the nation, from the Gulf of Mexico up to the Carolinas. In those humid areas the vapor retarder must be installed over the exterior sheathing rather than on the interior walls. In a narrow band above the "Humid Climate" is a "Fringe Climate," where no vapor retarder at all may be needed. Keep in mind that improper installation of a vapor retarder may cause extensive damage to the house structure. As noted in the Introduction, it is best to check with local contractors and building inspectors to learn the conventional building methods for your particular climate.

VAPOR RETARDERS IN CRAWL SPACES

In Chapter 3, Waterproofing an Existing/New Basement, the importance of having a

Adding a Ceiling Vapor Retarder

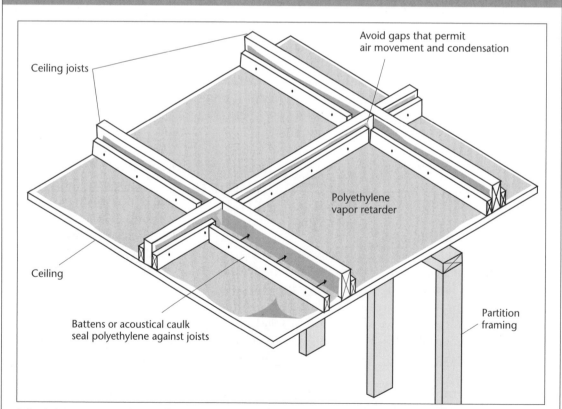

Ceiling joists

Avoid gaps that permit air movement and condensation

Polyethylene vapor retarder

Ceiling

Battens or acoustical caulk seal polyethylene against joists

Partition framing

Polyethylene vapor retarder installed in existing house. If attic insulation is installed, remove insulation before installing retarder.

Venting Soffits

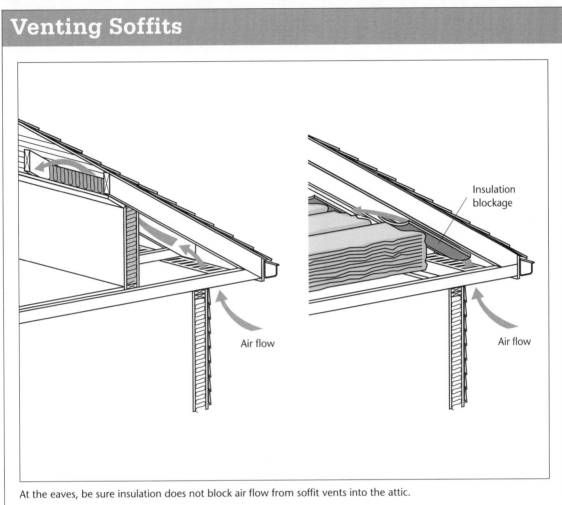

Insulation blockage

Air flow

Air flow

At the eaves, be sure insulation does not block air flow from soffit vents into the attic.

vapor retarder installed beneath the concrete basement floor was discussed. In houses that have a crawl space rather than a basement, it is also important to install a vapor retarder over the bare earth in the crawl space to prevent moisture migration from the soil. Crawl spaces should be built over well-drained soil, but even then moisture may migrate upward to cause a variety of problems within the crawl space.

First, install a vapor retarder over the bare soil. Because workers may be required to move about within the crawl space, the vapor retarder should be heavier than the 4-mil retarder recommended for use in walls. A 6-mil vapor retarder is generally considered adequate.

All seams in the vapor retarder should be overlapped by 6 inches (15 centimeters) and sealed. Use either tape or acoustical

sealant to seal the seams. At the perimeter of the foundation, fold the vapor retarder up 4 to 6 inches (10 to 15 centimeters) onto the foundation. Seal these edges with acoustical sealant.

When the vapor retarder is in place and sealed, spread a 2- to 3- inch (5- to 7.5- centimeters) layer of dry sand over the entire retarder. The sand will help hold the vapor retarder in place, retard vapor movement into the structure, and help

No Vapor Retarder

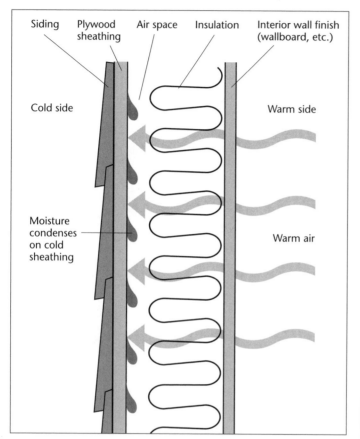

Siding   Plywood   Air space   Insulation   Interior wall finish
          sheathing   (wallboard, etc.)

Cold side   Warm side

Moisture
condenses   Warm air
on cold
sheathing

Moisture passes through interior wall and insulation and condenses on cold sheathing. Result: peeling paint, wet insulation.

prevent damage to the retarder when workers must move about in the crawl space.

From the crawl space side, install faced insulation batts between the floor joists. The facing should be a vapor retarder of either kraft paper or aluminum foil. The vapor retarder should be installed toward the warm side of the floor. Note that, for the same reasons explained in our dis-

cussion of ceiling vapor retarders, this procedure will not provide a continuous vapor retarder under the floor, because the vapor retarder is interrupted by having a joint at each floor joist.

In cold climates, install the insulation with the vapor retarder facing upward; in warm humid climates, install the insulation with the vapor retarder down. If the vapor retarder is

facing downward it can be overlapped and stapled over the bottom face of the floor joists, forming a better vapor retarder than when the retarder is installed with the facing up. (See page 70.)

As further insurance to help keep the crawl space area dry, ventilation of the space may be necessary. Again, the requirements depend on the area in which you live; in cold climates, year-round ventilation of the crawl space is required to permit moisture to migrate to the outdoors. In warm, humid climates, the outdoor air may be more humid than the air in the crawl space, so the moisture transfer will occur from the outdoors into the crawl space. Check with local building inspectors for ventilation requirements in your area.

AIR BARRIERS

As noted above, beside diffusion, moisture in the air can move through air leakage or convection. An air barrier bars the infiltration of outside air to the interior of the house, and bars the exfiltration of conditioned (heated or cooled) air from the interior to the exterior. Otherwise, water vapor in the air will move through the walls or ceiling. In fact, United States Gypsum in their Gypsum Construction Handbook estimates that more than 230 times as much moisture moves by air leaks or convection than by diffusion. So, an air barrier or combination vapor retarder/air barrier is essential to control convective air movement and vapor transfer.

There are three factors that affect the air pressure and its flow from inside out or from outside in. The first is the stack or chimney effect, which means that warm air rises and attempts to exit through the upper walls or the ceiling. In winter, as the warm air rises, it produces an outward pressure through the upper walls and ceiling, and creates a suction through the lower portions of the walls that pulls in cold exterior air. In summer, an air-conditioned house will produce a reversal of air pressures and flow direction.

The second factor in air convection is wind pressure on the exterior of the house. The outdoor air movement causes a positive pressure on the side of the house that faces the wind (the windward side). Thus air will infiltrate from the windward side, causing a suction pressure or exfiltration of air on the opposite (or leeward) side of the house. When determining the effect of wind pressure on a house, consider the height of the house, because a two- or

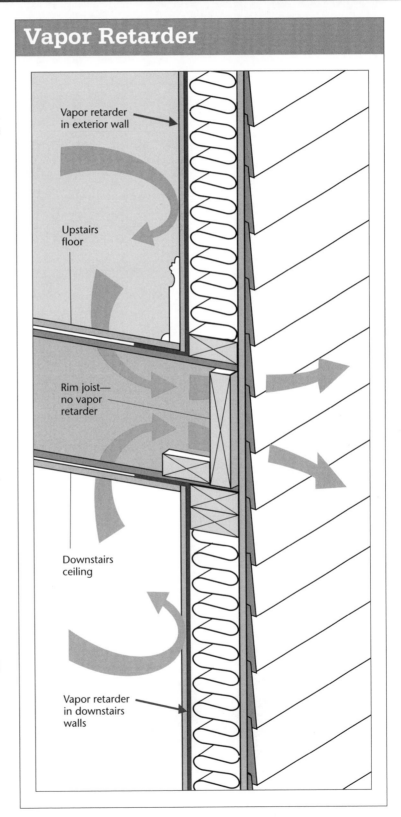

Vapor Retarder

Vapor retarder in exterior wall

Upstairs floor

Rim joist— no vapor retarder

Downstairs ceiling

Vapor retarder in downstairs walls

Vapor Retarder in Crawl Space: Cold Climate

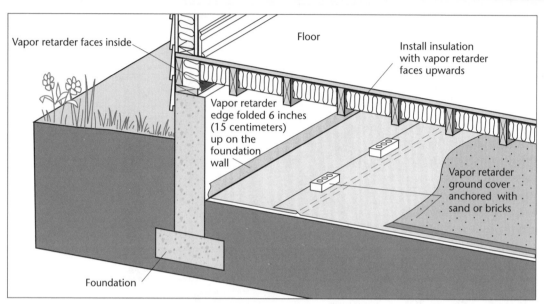

Vapor retarder faces inside

Floor

Install insulation with vapor retarder faces upwards

Vapor retarder edge folded 6 inches (15 centimeters) up on the foundation wall

Vapor retarder ground cover anchored with sand or bricks

Foundation

In cold climates, a ground vapor retarder prevents moisture from rising to the floor above: insulation has vapor retarder facing upwards.

Vapor Retarder in Crawl Space: Humid Climate

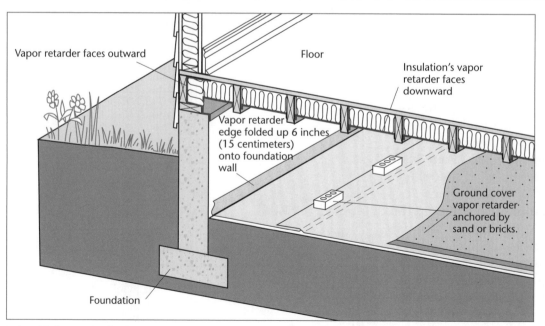

Vapor retarder faces outward

Floor

Insulation's vapor retarder faces downward

Vapor retarder edge folded up 6 inches (15 centimeters) onto foundation wall

Ground cover vapor retarder anchored by sand or bricks.

Foundation

In humid climates the floor vapor retarder is installed face downward.

three-story house will be subjected to the increased wind pressure at higher elevations.

To minimize the effects of unequal vapor pressure, pay careful attention to ensure there are no voids that permit moisture to be lost through the walls. When building a new house or addition, inspect the vapor retarder/air barrier installation after all other work is done, but before wallboard, plaster, or paneling is installed. Be sure that all seams in the polyethylene film are overlapped 6 inches (15 centimeters) and are sealed with tape or other acceptable sealants. This overlap is especially crucial at the corners where walls meet walls, or walls meet ceilings. All interruptions of the film at windows, doors, plumbing, heating or electrical outlets must be sealed in the same way.

CHAPTER 6
Home Humidity Problems

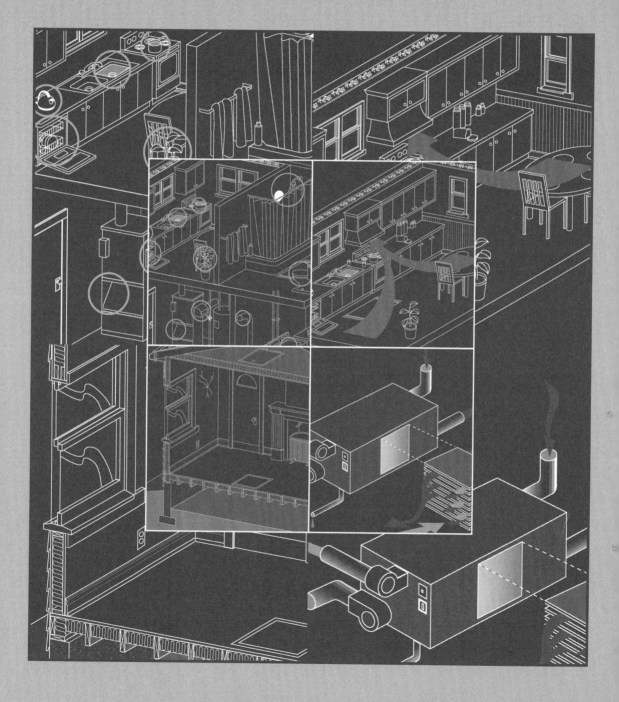

Whether too low or too high, indoor humidity can cause a variety of problems. When indoor humidity levels are low, human health may suffer. Dry, itchy skin, brittle hair, nasal and bronchial irritation, and shocks from static electricity are symptoms of low humidity levels. For maximum indoor comfort the Consumer Products Safety Commission suggests that the indoor humidity level be maintained at between 30 and 50 percent at 72 degrees Fahrenheit (22 degrees Celsius).

High indoor humidity is not a problem in drafty older houses, where humidity escapes through cracks around leaking doors and windows, and through walls and ceilings that contain no insulation or vapor retarder. Outdoor relative humidity averages much lower in seasons of cold weather and may go down to the 15 percent level, which is as dry as the Sahara Desert. In winter, it is often necessary to use a humidifier to maintain humidity at minimum comfort levels of between 30 and 50 percent.

As the emphasis on energy conservation has increased, building codes have become more strict, calling for increased levels of insulation and the use of continuous vapor retarders,

meaning vapor retarders in both walls and ceilings. To control vapor and heat loss, windows and doors have been engineered to increase their thermal performance, and to decrease the air infiltration rate.

To improve their thermal efficiency, many older houses have been retrofitted with improved weather-stripping, caulk, and insulation. This emphasis on better thermal efficiency has tightened houses against moisture migration to the point that the effect on occupants is somewhat comparable to living inside a plastic bag.

Many new houses do not require humidifiers; in fact, in many newer houses indoor humidity levels are too high for comfort. These higher humidity levels produce myriad problems, including mold, mildew, peeling paint, and damage to the house structure and furnishings.

In this chapter we will discuss both high and low humidity levels, and suggest ways to control indoor humidity levels, both to minimize damage to the house structure and to maintain maximum occupant comfort.

HIGH INDOOR HUMIDITY

High indoor humidity levels can produce damage to all

the components of a house, including window sashes, doors, trim, and wood framing. Too much humidity can virtually destroy the house itself. If you suspect that you may have high humidity levels, use the following list to carefully assess the entire house for symptoms of excess indoor humidity.

Symptoms of High Humidity

Dampness When indoor humidity is too high, there often is a pervasive feeling of dampness in the house, especially in closets, stored clothing, or furniture. Depending on the indoor ventilation and window quality at humidity levels above 40 percent, condensation or buildup of frost or ice on window glass may develop. To compromise between frost on window panes and personal comfort, reduce humidity levels to the point where moisture does not condense on window glass.

Odors Other symptoms of moisture buildup include the presence of mold or mildew and musty odors. (See Mildew below.)

Warped Wood When wet, wood trim or siding may expand and deform, then crack or warp during dry

Home Moisture Sources

Home humidity is raised by cooking, bath activities, stored firewood, heating equipment, laundry, and potted plants.

weather. Dark brown, black, or green stains indicate mildew, while gray or yellow stains with web-like lines indicate moisture-borne fungi. These symptoms may be found on either wet or dry wood, or beneath carpets, behind furniture, or on concrete foundations.

Wood Rot/Decay Knock on wood: sound wood will have a sharp ring, while soft wood will yield a dull thud when struck. Wood that is rotted by moisture will usually be soft and easy to penetrate with a sharp tool. Use a sharp carpenter's awl or ice pick to probe wood framing. Probe any wood that looks suspicious, with emphasis on the mud sills (the flat wood member that meets the top of the foundation wall), the rim or band joists that sit atop the mud sills, and all the floor joists, particularly at the point where the floor joists meet the rim joists. The sharp probe will easily penetrate any decayed or rotted wood, while wood that is sound will resist penetration.

Plumbing Check the entire plumbing system for leaks or dripping faucets (see Chapter 8, Leaking Plumbing). If humidity levels are too high, vapor may condense on cold-water supply pipes or on the toilet bowl.

New Construction During new construction, hundreds of gallons (liters) of water may be used in a house interior. This water is contained in concrete, drywall materials, and paint, among other things. A single kiln-dried 2 × 4 stud may contain 1 cup (250 milliliters) of water, so there is a huge amount of water contained in the framing lumber.

During the settling period, all the interior moisture will escape into the air and exit the structure. To avoid moisture and shrinkage problems, the best time to build your new house is during warm, dry weather. After pouring the concrete basement slab, allow it to cure for at least one week before starting the drywall finishing. This will prevent moisture buildup during the construction period, and you will move into a house that has already exhausted most of the moisture introduced during construction.

Wet Basements Damp or wet basement walls or any other sign of water entry into the building will contribute to a buildup of excess moisture in the house. (See Chapter 3, Waterproofing a Basement.)

Masonry Problems
Efflorescence is a powdery, white to gray substance that may leach out of concrete when moisture is present. Chipped or crumbling concrete and/or a buildup of efflorescence on basement walls usually indicates the presence of moisture.

Evaporation Evaporative moisture is added to the house interior when standing water evaporates from house plants, aquariums, sewer drains, drainage sumps, or toilet bowls that are left uncovered. Keep covers in place over drains or sumps, and leave the lid down on the toilet bowl.

Appliances Gas-fired heating, water-heating, and cooking appliances produce water vapor during the combustion process. This moisture production is increased when the appliances are not properly cleaned and adjusted. Unvented kerosene heaters also produce moisture during combustion, and firewood can give off moisture both during indoor storage and during combustion.

It is a poor idea to vent a clothes dryer into the basement or other laundry area. This practice was a common one generated during the oil embargo to conserve energy use. But a clothes dryer is run sporadically and only a few hours per week, so the heat saved is a very minor gain. In an effort to conserve this small amount of heat, gallons (liters) of water are released from electric or gas dryers into the house. In addition to moisture, gas dryers also vent dangerous combustion gases into the house. Both types of dryers emit lint and chemicals such as bleach and detergents. Vent any clothes dryer, either gas or electric, to the outside. Basement laundry rooms should also be equipped with an exhaust vent of at least 50 cubic feet per minute (4 cubic meters).

Lack of Ventilation Most of the moisture produced by family activities is generated in the kitchen, the bath, and the laundry. Therefore, exhaust fans and vents should be installed in each of these areas. Gas ranges may be unvented, so they give off moisture into the living space. Even though a range hood may be present, there may be no vapor exhaust to the exterior. Some range hood vents are charcoal filters that only catch grease and filter air, and do not exhaust moisture to the outdoors. Other range vent hoods are exhausted into the attic, where the moisture and grease may be trapped, causing a variety of problems. Correct venting so it exhausts moisture outside, not into the attic. The exhaust vents should have

the capacity to move a minimum of 100 cubic feet of air per minute (cfm) in the kitchen, and 50 cfm in the bathroom or laundry.

Vapor Retarder In houses that have no vapor retarder, or a poorly installed vapor retarder, moisture can pass through the wall or ceiling either by diffusion or through air leakage or convection. When this occurs, moisture can condense on either ceiling or wall insulation, thus greatly reducing the R-value of the insulation. This moisture can also cause damage to plaster or wallboard, promote the growth of mildew or mold, and cause dry rot in the framing. (Dry rot is a misnomer, because dry rot is caused by moisture.) As mentioned in Chapter 5, Vapor Retarders, you can create a vapor retarder by applying a coat of alkyd sealer or paint to the ceilings and to the interior side of exterior walls.

Insulation Voids Any void in the insulation can be a potential trouble spot for moisture buildup. Especially during the heating season, moisture may be seen as wet spots at the juncture or corner where exterior walls meet the ceiling. This is caused by moisture condensation on a cold spot or point where the insulation blankets in the ceiling do

not overlap at the top plate of the wall. The remedy is to extend the ceiling insulation so it overlaps the top plate of the wall but does not block the flow of air from the soffits into the attic.

Temperature Differences Moisture may condense where air movement is restricted by furniture or drapes that are set against exterior walls, or in closets or in rooms that are closed off and unheated. The remedy is to set furniture away from the wall so air can circulate evenly throughout the house. Also, do not close off an unused room. Because of the spillover effect of heat through the uninsulated interior walls, the potential savings in energy costs from closing a room is small. To the extent that the surfaces in the closed-off room are cooled, the potential for condensation and moisture damage is increased.

Indoor Plants Live plants must be watered, and they will in turn release moisture into the air. If you have many plants, they may be contributing to high indoor humidity levels. Five to seven average plants can generate as much as 1 pint (500 milliliters) of water per day.

Greenhouses or sunrooms that are attached to

the house can cause problems when many plants produce high moisture levels and may require ventilation or dehumidification. Unless the common wall between the house and greenhouse is protected with a vapor retarder, the vapor from the greenhouse may migrate into the common wall, causing condensation and moisture problems inside the wall.

Exterior Moisture Problems The siding on the house must never be in contact with the ground, or rain or snow from the ground will enter the siding and cause it to warp or rot.

Shrubs or trees that shade the house may also reduce air circulation over the exterior, so the exterior surfaces stay constantly damp. The dampness will promote the growth of mildew or mold, and will also cause wood rot. Trim trees and shrubs to allow sunlight and air circulation to dry the exterior surfaces. Do not store firewood or other materials against the house where they obstruct air flow and may trap moisture. Inspect the roof and soffit vents and clean them if they are plugged with leaves or other debris to ensure proper circulation.

Peeling Paint High humidity levels can cause paint to peel on either interior or exterior surfaces. Peeling or alligatored paint caused by humidity is common in bathrooms and kitchens. In extreme cases, a vaporizer or humidifier can cause the paint to peel in that room.

When interior humidity levels rise, interior vapor pressure will cause the humidity to attempt to equalize with exterior humidity levels. If there are no vapor retarders, the moisture-laden air will flow through the exterior walls and will peel the paint on the siding. If there are convective air leaks around window and door openings, the moisture will escape around these voids and will peel the trim paint. This peeling trim paint is commonly seen on stucco or brick houses, where the path of least resistance to moisture passage is around the windows and doors. Caulk all cracks around interior trim to seal against moisture.

If the moisture passes through the ceilings into the attic, paint may peel on soffits, fascia boards, or gable ends of the house. (Refer to "Roof Waterproofing" illustration on page 47.)

Moisture will peel paint at any point where a crack allows water entry. One common point for exterior peeling paint is at the base of porch posts or pillars, where wood posts meet concrete floors. The water will wick up into the unpainted end grain, causing the paint to peel. Use pressure-treated wood for posts or pillars. Seal the ends of the posts before installation, then caulk cracks where post ends meet concrete.

CONTROLLING INTERIOR HUMIDITY LEVELS

Nature will determine exterior humidity levels, but there is much that can be done to control interior humidity levels. Interior moisture levels affect both the structure of the house and the comfort of the occupants, so it is important to try to hold indoor humidity between 30 and 50 percent when the indoor temperature is 72 degrees Fahrenheit (22 degrees Celsius). In this section we will review methods to control interior humidity levels.

MOISTURE SOURCES

To determine if your interior humidity levels are too high (see Symptoms of High Humidity above), thoroughly review all sources of moisture so you can institute appropriate controls.

The first step is to understand how much moisture is generated by family activities. For example,

Whole-House Ventilation

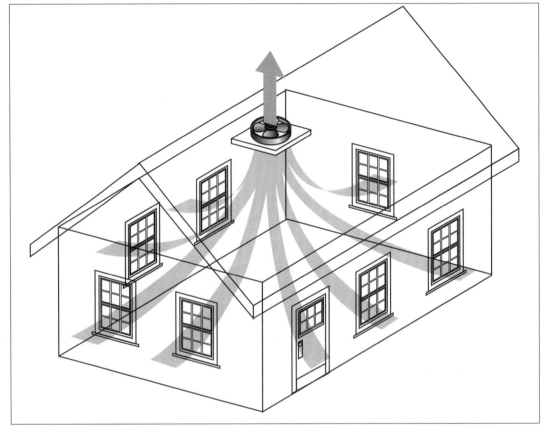

A whole-house fan can cool the house and remove stale/humid air.

mopping a 100-square-foot (3-square-meters) floor will add 3 pints (1.5 liters) of water vapor to the interior, while a five-minute shower can contribute ½ pint (250 milliliters) of water to the air. Cooking dinner on a gas range for a family of four can add 1-¼ pints (625 milliliters) daily, and frost-free refrigerators add a pint (500 milliliters) of water per day through the defrost cycle. Burning an unvented kerosene space heater can add 7.6 pints (2 liters) of water per gallon (4 liters) of kerosene burned. In a faulty furnace, combustion exhaust gas backdrafting or spillage can add a whopping 840 gallons (3,360 liters) of water per year. The humidity gain from each of these activities can be controlled or eliminated. For examples of how water-vapor is generated see page 74.

WHOLE HOUSE HUMIDITY CONTROL

Humidity problems and remedies vary widely by geographic region. Always contact local building experts and follow standard building practices for your area. Your goal is to move interior humidity so it can equalize with outdoor humidity levels. The advice offered above applies to perhaps three-quarters

Kitchen Ventilation

A hood vent in the kitchen exhausts odors and removes excess moisture.

of the continental U.S.

However, if outdoor humidity levels are high, no humidity can transfer from the interior to the exterior. Remember that vapor pressure or humidity transfer is always from the highest level to the lowest level, so if outdoor humidity is a problem, the moisture transfer from venting or exhausting air may be from outdoors in rather than from indoors out. This problem is most common in the states along the southeastern coast of the U.S.

Appliances

If you have gas-fired appliances, combustion of natural gas can add humidity to the indoors. Be sure that vents are open and that burners are properly adjusted. If combustion air is inadequate, a yellow or wavy flame at the burner can signal incomplete combustion and moisture generation, as well as danger from combus-

tion gases such as carbon monoxide. Each year, at the beginning of the heating season, have a professional technician inspect and adjust any gas-fired furnace or water heater. Have your furnace fitted with a duct to supply outdoor air for combustion.

Unvented space heaters can also add to indoor humidity levels. As mentioned, an unvented kerosene heater can add almost 1 gallon (4 liters) of

Bath Ventilation

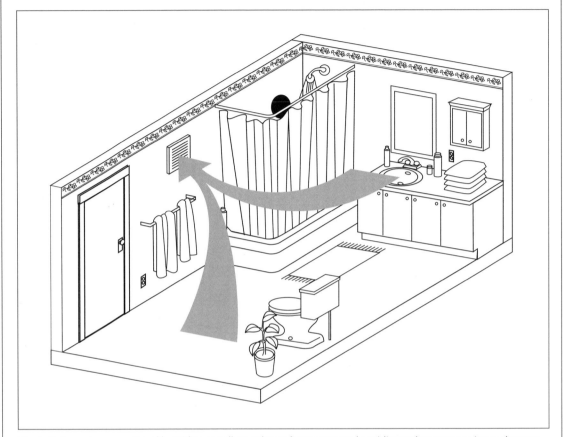

The bath is a primary source of humidity. Install an exhaust fan to remove humidity and prevent moisture damage.

water for each gallon (4 liters) of kerosene burned. In addition, operating any unvented appliance that burns fossil fuel presents a carbon monoxide hazard. Never use any unvented fossil-fuel space heater in the house. Kerosene space heaters present carbon monoxide risks and are therefore too dangerous for use.

Firewood adds humidity to indoor air during indoor storage and combustion. Buy only well-seasoned firewood, store it outdoors under cover so it can dry out during storage, and close fireplace doors to prevent moisture from entering the living space. Equip wood-burning stoves or fireplaces with outdoor combustion air ducts.

Years ago, gas ranges were exempted from venting code requirements, the theory being that they were operated only occasionally and for limited time periods. Nevertheless, in a tightly built house there is a real danger of carbon monoxide poisoning if an unvented gas range is run for a long period, such as in preparation of a family holiday meal, or to supplement space heating. Never use any gas range for supplemental space heating. Equip the range with a hood exhaust vent that has a capacity to move 100 cubic feet per minute of air (100 cfm or 9 cubic meters), and exhausts the air to the outdoors. When

Moisture Transfer

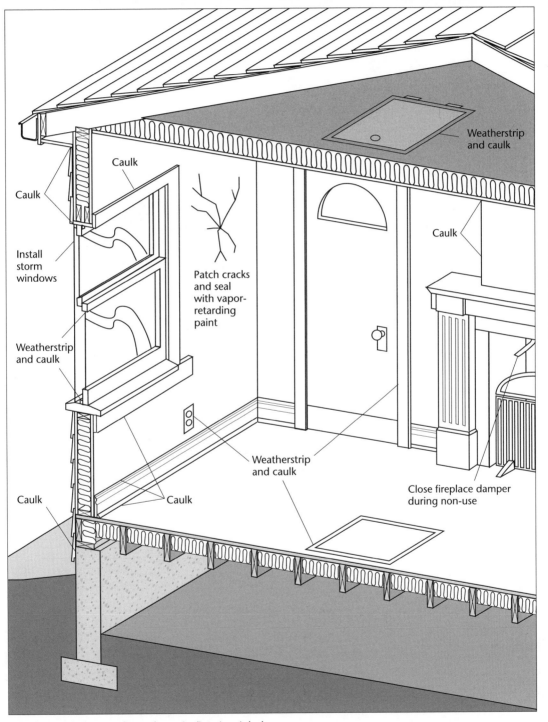

Caulk

Caulk

Install storm windows

Weatherstrip and caulk

Caulk

Patch cracks and seal with vapor-retarding paint

Weatherstrip and caulk

Caulk

Caulk

Weatherstrip and caulk

Weatherstrip and caulk

Caulk

Close fireplace damper during non-use

To reduce moisture transfer, seal exterior/interior air leaks.

High Humidity

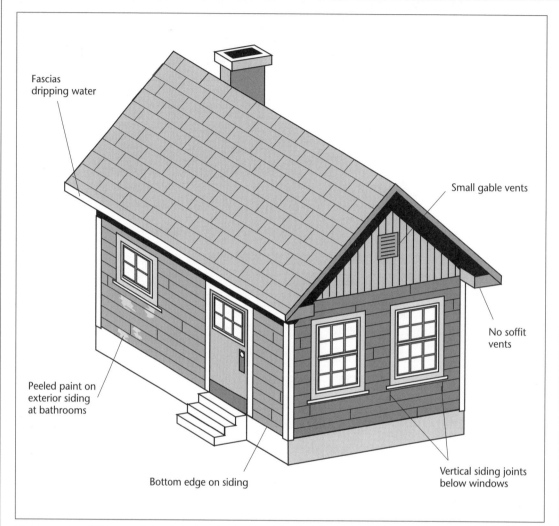

Fascias dripping water

Small gable vents

No soffit vents

Peeled paint on exterior siding at bathrooms

Bottom edge on siding

Vertical siding joints below windows

High home humidity can ruin insulation, peel paint, and rot siding, windows, and house framing.

stove filters, use lids to cover cooking utensils and minimize moisture loss into the air.

Plumbing

Plumbing problems can add to indoor humidity levels. Leaking pipes, faucets, or drains all contribute moisture and should be repaired immediately. Inspect and replace faulty drain traps or rusty steel traps under sink drains or tubs. To control evaporation, drainage sumps should have a cover, but many people fail to keep the cover in place. To limit evaporation, cover sumps and floor drains, and keep the toilet seat down.

Another source of interior humidity is condensation on plumbing pipes or fixtures. Buy and install tubular foam insulation for water supply pipes. Condensation, caused by cold water being pumped into the bowl each time the toilet is flushed, is also common on toilet bowls and tanks. This cold water cools the bowl and tank, and warm moist air meeting the cold toilet fixture condenses on its surface. To prevent toilet condensation, cover the fixture with a terrycloth cover, insulate the toilet tank (Styrofoam tank insulation kits are available at home centers), or install a mixing valve that will mix hot and cold water for delivery to the toilet tank. Warm water from the mixing valve will not cool the toilet fixture, so there will be no condensation.

Potpourri

A tub bath adds only about one-quarter as much moisture to the air as a shower does. Low-flow shower heads control water usage but, because they atomize the water, they add more moisture to the air than ordinary showerheads.

After bathing and drying yourself, use the towel to wipe down the tile or fiberglass shower enclosure, wipe moisture off any shower doors or mirrors, and run the exhaust fan to exhaust the moisture from the bathroom. Don't leave wet towels in a clothes hamper; immediately remove wet towels or bath mats from the bathroom and place them in the clothes dryer so the moisture will be vented outdoors. To improve air flow and reduce humidity,

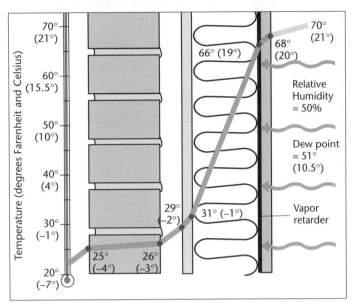

Wall Moisture—Cold Climates

In cold climates moisture will condense on brick veneer if there is no vapor retarder on the warm side of the wall.

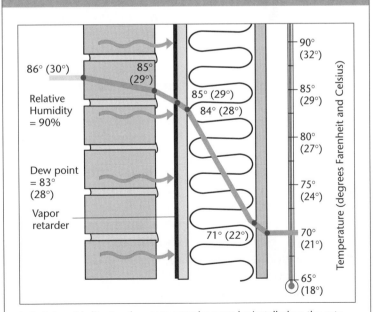

Wall Moisture: Humid Climate

In hot, humid climates the vapor retarder must be installed on the exterior sheathing.

clean air registers and cold air return covers, replace furnace filters monthly, and have air ducts cleaned by professionals at least every two years.

To improve air circulation, install louvered closet doors, wire shelves, and storage baskets in closets.

Desiccants are chemicals that absorb moisture from the air. Nontoxic chemical desiccants, like silica gel or activated alumina, can be placed in any area where moisture is present, such as a damp closet or basement. Place the desiccants in a porous or open container, such as a paper bag. The desiccants mentioned above can be reused; when the material is saturated with moisture, place the desiccant in a 300 degree Fahrenheit (150 degree Celsius) oven for several hours to remove the moisture. Another method to reduce closet humidity is to leave a small light bulb on in the closet.

In climates where low outdoor humidity levels are common, there is no better way to remove moisture from a house than simply opening the windows and letting the house air out. Damp, musty basements often have windows that have not been opened for years, some are even painted shut. Open the windows at opposite ends of the basement and place a fan facing outside at one window. This will promote cross ventilation, and stale, damp basement air will be exhausted.

MILDEW

Mildew is a fungus growth that can produce objectionable odors and destroy a house and its contents. Mildew and its source must be addressed, because mildew may be the first signal that more serious problems lurk in the house.

To grow and flourish, mildew spores require heat, darkness, moisture, and poor air circulation. Where there is little air circulation along walls, such as in closets and behind furniture and drapes, check for dark stains that may indicate mildew. These stains often are visible on the walls at corners, or at base trim levels.

To remove mildew, use chlorine bleach (see dilution proportions below) or a disinfectant to kill the spores. Then reduce the humidity levels and permit fresh air to circulate throughout the house. Below are specific tips for removing mildew from interior surfaces and furnishings.

Walls and Ceilings

Mix 1 or 2 cups (250 to 500 milliliters) of chlorine bleach in a gallon (4 liters) of water. Wear eye protection, rubber gloves, and old clothes when handling bleach products, and cover all furniture, drapes, and carpets.

If mildew is widespread, use a sponge to apply the bleach/water mixture to the walls, ceilings, or wood or vinyl floors. Let the solution sit on the surface for a few minutes, then wipe away the mildew spores with a clean cloth and rinse with plain water. If this does not remove the mildew, repeat the procedure, using an additional 1 cup (250 milliliters) of bleach to the mixture. For small areas of mildew, pour the bleach/water solution into a spray bottle and spray the affected area. Use the same bleach/water solution to clean concrete basement walls. If you have a large area to cover, use a sponge mop to apply the solution. Let set a few minutes, then rinse with clear water.

Windows and Doors

Water stains or mildew may form on doors or windows. Some woods such as oak will develop black stains due to the tannic acid in the wood. Try the bleach solution mentioned above on any black stains on doors or windows; if the stains are mildew, the bleach solution will remove them. If not, use oxalic acid to bleach out the stains, following the manufacturer's instructions.

Decay and Rot Areas

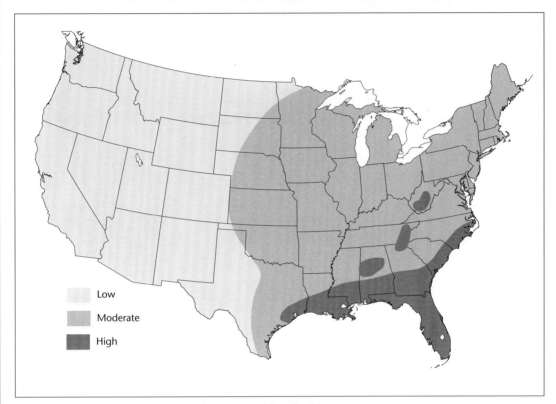

Low

Moderate

High

High humidity areas are prone to wood decay, rot, mold, and mildew.

Upholstered Furniture

Move mildewed upholstered furniture or mattresses outdoors to air out. Sunlight is best, but may fade furniture colors, so place colored furnishings in the shade for a full day. Vacuum the furniture or mattress thoroughly, then wipe down with a cloth dampened with a 50:50 solution of denatured alcohol and water. Try an inconspicuous spot first. Let the items dry completely. If odors remain, contact a professional fumigating service.

Wood Furniture

Place mildewed wood furniture outside in a shaded area; direct sunlight may cause the wood to warp or split. Remove drawers from dressers or desks. Use a bleach solution to remove the mildew, then rinse. Lightly sand the unfinished portions. When the furniture is completely dry seal and deodorize the bare wood. Mix ⅓ cup (75 milliliters) of cedar oil, (available at furniture stores or drugstores) with ⅔ cup (160 milliliters) of water. Use a small foam

paint brush or a clean cloth to apply the cedar oil/water mix to the unfinished wood such as the bottom and insides of drawers.

Clothing, Drapes, and Carpets

To remove mildew, take drapes and clothes to a dry cleaner. For washable clothes or fabrics, hang them in the sunlight and let them air out for a full day, or until odor free. Then wash the clothes as instructed on the labels, using a bleach that is fabric safe. Have

Winter Condensation

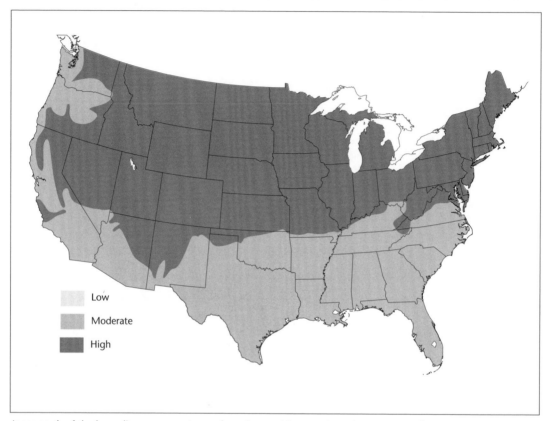

Low

Moderate

High

Areas north of the lower line are prone to condensation problems and require vapor retarders.

carpets and rugs professionally cleaned.

If a shower curtain is mildewed, soak it in a tub with hot water and chlorine bleach (2–3 cups/500–700 milliliters) of bleach to tub of water. Plastic curtains cannot be damaged by bleach; ensure that curtains made of other fabric can tolerate bleach. After soaking the curtain to kill mildew spores, wash it in the machine and hang it in the sunlight to dry.

Siding, Outdoor Structures

How-to texts often refer to the natural graying of unfinished woods such as cedar or redwood. This gray patina in fact is dirt or mildew. To remove mildew from exterior siding, fences, decks, or retaining walls, mix 1 quart (1 liter) of bleach with 1 gallon (4 liters) of water. Pre-wet the wood with clear water, then use a pump-type garden sprayer or paint sprayer to apply the bleach solution to the surfaces. Let

sit for five minutes, then use a hose nozzle or power washer to blast away the grime and mildew. Flush all treated surfaces well to remove the bleach. To prevent mildew recurrence, apply a clear wood sealer to the wood when the wood is dry.

The bleach/water solution is inexpensive and is safe for flowers and lawn. If you prefer, there are commercial wood cleaners such as Dekswood that are guaranteed to be environmentally safe.

DEHUMIDIFYING

In addition to using natural solutions such as ventilation to remove moisture from indoor air, mechanical options are available. These mechanical devices include dehumidifiers, whole-house fans, and air-to-air heat exchangers.

Dehumidifiers

Mechanical dehumidifiers are portable appliances with humidistat switch, that will turn them on when humidity reaches a preset level.

Most dehumidifiers are refrigerator types that cool the air to condense and remove the moisture. The humid air is pulled into the appliance and flows across refrigerator coils. The refrigerator coils are colder than the dew point, so the humidity condenses on the coils and runs down into a catch basin or pan. There is a float shutoff that turns the appliance off when the pan is full. Remove the pan to manually empty the collected water, or attach a hose to the basin so that the collected water flows directly into a floor drain. Dehumidifiers are available in a variety of capacities, and your dealer can help you select the right one for your needs.

Whole-House Fans

Whole-house fans are large fans that are installed in the ceiling at a central point in the house, such as in a center hall ceiling. Whole-house fans will both cool the house interior and also remove indoor humidity, assuming the exterior air is less humid than the interior air and moisture transfer can occur.

The theory behind the whole-house fan is that in all but the warmest climates, outdoor air at night will be cooler than indoor air. The system works best when the lowest windows in the house are opened during cool nighttime hours. Then the fan pulls in the coolest ground-level air and exhausts the warm, stale air from the interior upward into the attic. The warmer air then exits the attic through roof or gable vents, and more cool outside air is pulled in behind it. In this way the entire interior of the house and its contents are cooled to outdoor or ambient temperatures, and excess moisture is removed with the warm air.

To prevent solar heat gain during the heat of the day, at sunrise the fan is shut off and house windows and drapes are closed. Even in hot climates, in a properly insulated house the interior heat rise will be only about 1 degree Fahrenheit (0.55° Celsius) per hour, so the house will remain cool throughout the day. In all but the hottest climates this system can be substituted for more expensive air conditioning equipment.

There is much industry confusion regarding the capacity of the fan needed to accomplish whole-house ventilation. According to the American Ventilation Association (AVA), a whole-house fan should have a capacity large enough to achieve one air change per minute. To calculate the fan capacity needed for your house, multiply the square footage of the house by the ceiling height. For example, a house having 1,200 square feet (133 square meters) of floor space × the standard 8-foot (2.5-meter) ceiling height = 9,600 cubic feet (1,060 cubic meters) of air. The whole house fan should thus have a capacity of 9,600 cfm (1,060 square meters per minute).

Air-to-Air Heat Exchangers

Any house that is located in a cold climate, and is tightly built with a continuous (wall and ceiling) vapor barrier, may need an air-to-air heat exchanger. These exchangers have ducts to both the interior and the exterior: the ducts pass each other in the unit and the heat from the exhausted air is transferred to the incoming air, thus conserving energy. Some exchangers do not remove airborne moisture in this

Heat Exchanger

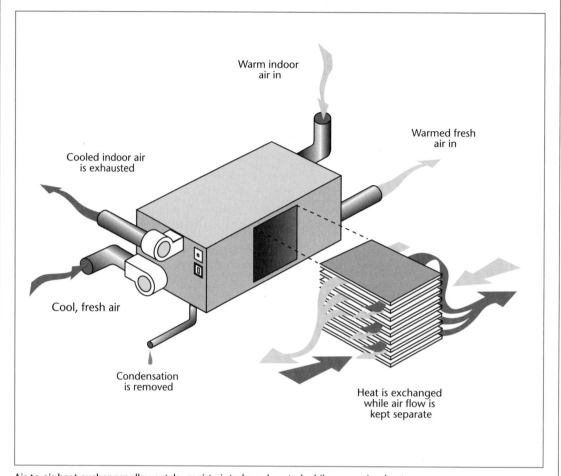

Warm indoor
air in

Warmed fresh
air in

Cooled indoor air
is exhausted

Cool, fresh air

Condensation
is removed

Heat is exchanged
while air flow is
kept separate

Air-to-air heat exchanger allows stale, moist air to be exhausted while recovering heat.

process, so be sure to select a unit that meets your needs.

For best performance, an air-to-air heat exchanger should be ducted to all rooms. Because ventilation and air circulation is constant, slightly higher indoor humidity can be tolerated in houses with exchangers.

Small heat exchangers are available as substitutes for exhaust fans in the bathroom or kitchen and can be mounted on walls or ceilings.

HUMIDIFIERS

If you live in an arid climate, you may need to add indoor humidity to ensure personal comfort. Signs of too-low humidity include shrinkage of wood components such as trim. If this occurs, miter joints at the corners of doors or window trim may open

and crack; furniture joints may loosen, and cracks may develop in plaster or wallboard. Personal discomfort from low humidity may be due to shocks from static electricity, dry skin, and brittle hair, and nasal or bronchial distress.

Mechanical humidifiers include two basic types: those that are mounted in the ductwork of forced-air heating systems, and separate appliances that can easily be moved about the house.

The type and size of humidifier needed depends on the average relative humidity in your area, plus the size of the space to be humidified. Determine the area of your house in cubic feet (or meters) (length × width × ceiling height) and take this figure to your local dealer. He or she will help you choose the right size humidifier for your needs.

Depending on its capacity, a mechanical humidifier can add up to 20 gallons (80 liters) of water to the home's interior each day. The average humidifier will add about 3 gallons (12 liters) per day. But seven average house plants can add 1 pint (500 milliliters) of water to the air per day; dishwashing, bathing, and cooking can add 4 pints (1 liter) or more per day, and drying clothes indoors can add 5 to 6 pints (2.5 to 3 liters) per load. The moisture generated by these activities and others, while undesirable in a tightly built house, may add needed humidity to houses in arid climates.

CHAPTER 7

Windows and Doors

indows and doors are particularly vulnerable to moisture problems. Both are built in rough openings framed into the walls. These openings are built slightly larger than the prefabricated window or door units that will be installed inside them to permit the carpenter to adjust or to level and plumb the units in the rough openings. These openings interrupt both the insulation blankets and the vapor retarders in the walls, and can create thermal or air/moisture leaks in the house. If the vapor retarder is not carefully sealed to the window or door frame, both heat and moisture can pass through these interruptions, and moisture damage can result. As noted in Chapter 5, Vapor Retarders, the retarder should be sealed to the window or door frame using a recommended sealant such as acoustic caulk.

Following the energy crisis of the late '70s, window manufacturers improved technology to produce windows that are vastly superior to older models. By using better materials and construction techniques, manufacturers have produced windows with improved thermal and air infiltration

Storm (Combination) Window

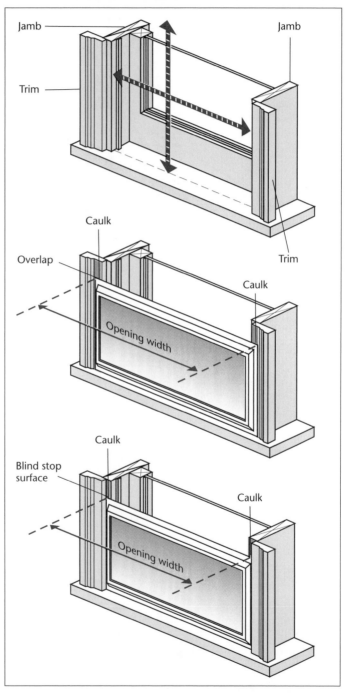

To install combination windows, measure the height and width of the window. The window may be installed inside the jambs (top illustration) or overlapped as shown (lower illustration.)

New Window Technology

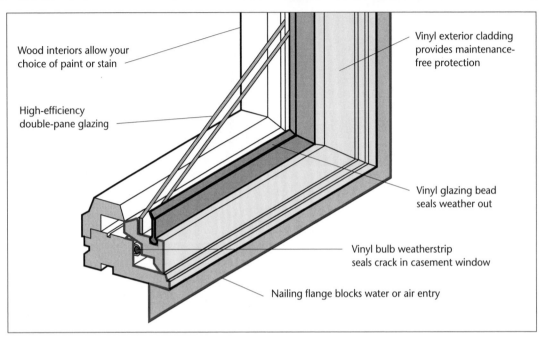

Wood interiors allow your choice of paint or stain

High-efficiency double-pane glazing

Vinyl exterior cladding provides maintenance-free protection

Vinyl glazing bead seals weather out

Vinyl bulb weatherstrip seals crack in casement window

Nailing flange blocks water or air entry

Window Installation

1. Check rough opening to be sure it is level, square, and plumb.

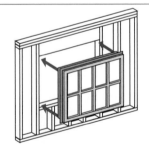

2. Center window in the opening and shim as needed.

3. Level the window and nail through flange.

4. Insulate the interior crack between the window and rough frame.

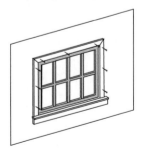

5. Apply interior window trim.

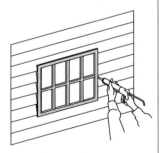

6. Caulk around the exterior of the window.

New window design provides for easy installation.

ratings. The manufacturer's close-tolerance construction and improved weather-stripping of new window models can also reduce air infiltration rates around moving window sashes.

Use of transparent films has reduced conductive heat loss through the glass, and insulating or double-pane glass now has argon or other thermally efficient gases—rather than trapped air—between the sealed panes. Because of such advances, modern windows are not the thermal leaks they once were, and houses built over the past decade likely have highly efficient windows. Still, for reasons we have outlined above, installation of windows in walls can create problems.

When building or remodeling, for greater energy efficiency, select the best quality windows and, to avoid moisture problems, have an experienced tradesperson install the windows.

Windows may be single pane or double pane, called insulating glass. In cold climates a second unit, called a storm window, may be installed on the outside of the primary window unit. These storm windows are called self-storing because they incorporate both screens and glass panes that can be closed to provide double-pane efficiency in cold weather.

Because glass itself is a poor insulator, either type of window has a low R-value relative to the insulated wall, and the glass panes will be cool in winter, often cool enough to permit humidity to condense on the glass. The moisture generated by this vapor condensation can run down the glass and wet the wood frames, or may run over the window sill and down the wall to cause moisture damage to the wallboard or plaster. During this process, the moisture that collects on the wood sash or sill can peel the varnish or polyurethane finish, stain the wood black, and, in extreme cases, promote wood decay and ruin the window unit.

To refinish a peeled or stained window sash or sill, use sandpaper or a scraper to remove the peeled finish. Then use oxalic acid to bleach the wood and remove the stains. Oxalic acid, a bleaching product, is available in crystal form at paint or home center stores. Mix the acid with water, following the manufacturer's directions, and apply by soaking a clean cloth in the mixture and laying the cloth on the stain. Repeat as necessary until the stain has disappeared and the natural wood color is restored, then rinse with clean water. Restain as necessary to match the rest of the

window finish. To protect against future staining, use spar (marine) varnish or a tough polyurethane product to refinish the damaged area.

To prevent or limit condensation on the window pane or glass, you must either warm the pane or lower the indoor humidity. To ensure that the glass pane stays relatively warm, choose high-efficiency windows. Also, if indoor humidity levels are controlled and air circulation is constant, moving air will reduce moisture condensation on the glass pane.

If you use a humidifier, adjust the humidity dial to produce a comfortable moisture level while limiting the condensation on window panes. During cold weather, turn the humidifier up gradually until visible condensation begins to form on the window. Then turn the humidifier control back gradually until the condensation is no longer visible on the panes.

If condensation forms on exterior storm panes, between the primary and storm windows, that is evidence that the drafty primary window is permitting airborne moisture to leak into the space between the windows. At the bottom or sill edge of the storm windows are "weep" holes that permit moisture to escape outside from the space

Roof Curb

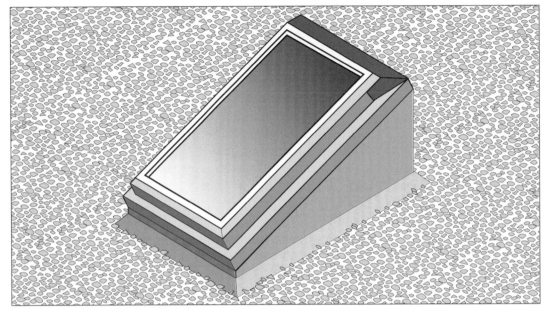

This roof curb is required when installing a skylight on a roof with a slope less than 15 degrees (3/12).

Curb-Mounted Fixed Skylight

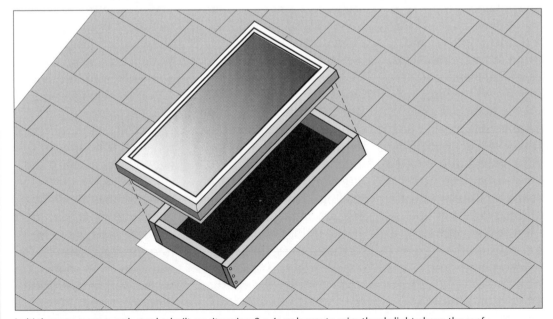

In high-snow areas, a curb can be built on site using 2 x 4s or larger to raise the skylight above the roof.

Double-Pane Glass

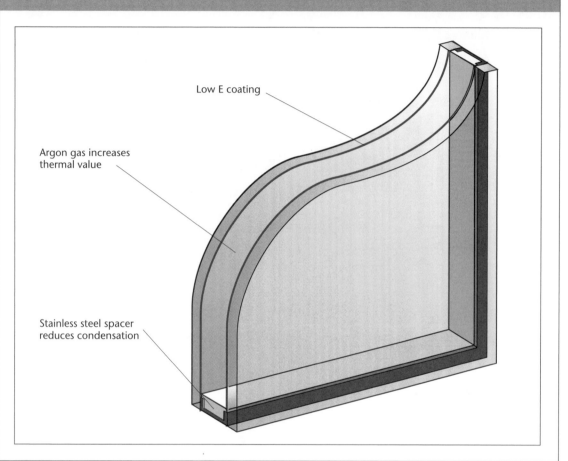

Low E coating

Argon gas increases thermal value

Stainless steel spacer reduces condensation

between the windows. Inspect the weep holes for dirt buildup, and use a straightened wire clothes hanger to clean them. Or open the storm sash periodically to allow the moisture that is trapped in the space between the windows to escape. If cleaning the weep holes does not eliminate condensation on the storm windows, either install new weather-stripping on the primary windows or replace the old primary windows with new, efficient models.

Double-pane or insulating glass windows are often not operable, but are fixed in the familiar "picture window" installation. These double panes are sealed at the perimeter so air or moisture cannot enter the space between the panes. In time, the perimeter seal may develop a leak and moisture may enter between the panes, causing a fogged window in cold weather. No repair is possible; the only solution is to install a new double-pane unit. If the window is still under manufacturer's warranty, ask for a replacement unit.

Peeling Paint on Window Trim

As noted above, there are interruptions in the insulation and vapor retarder at all window and door locations. In the majority of houses the vapor barrier is not sealed to the window or door frame, so the path of least resistance for moisture migration is through the gaps around the window or door frames.

New Vinyl Window

New window design ensures energy efficiency, no maintenance, and tilt-in design for easy cleaning.

As the moisture flows around the window and door frames, it will penetrate through the wall assembly to the exterior trim, where the paint on the trim forms a barrier to moisture passage. However, vapor pressure is so great that it will lift or peel the paint finish on the window or door trim, and may cause decay or rot in the component itself.

If you have peeling exterior trim paint, first try to reduce moisture penetration into window openings from the inside. Use an acrylic latex caulk to seal any cracks between the interior wall and trim. Next, apply a coat of alkyd sealer to the interior walls to create a surface vapor retarder. Finally, paint the wall with the finish coating of your choice.

Wearing a dust mask and goggles, scrape or sand the peeling exterior areas to remove the failing paint.

Old-Style Double-Hung Window

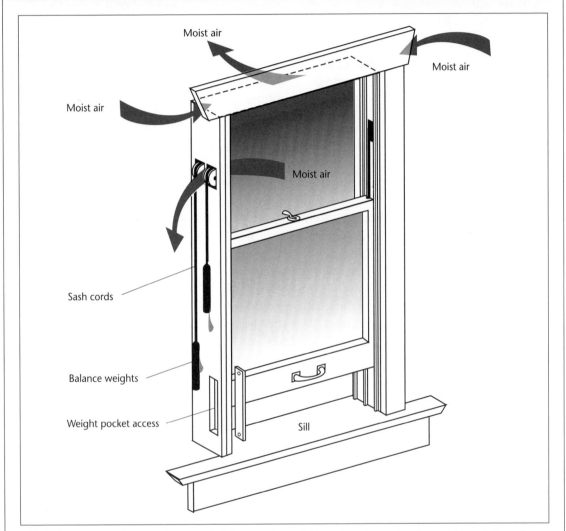

Moist air

Moist air

Moist air

Moist air

Sash cords

Balance weights

Weight pocket access

Sill

Old double-hung windows can be upgraded. Remove the weights and cords, insulate the weight pockets, and install spring clips to hold the sash in position.

Often, the bond between paint and trim fails over a wide surface, beyond the obviously peeling areas. To prevent future peeling of the new paint coat, scrape beyond the obviously failed areas onto sound paint to be sure that all loose paint has been removed.

When failing paint is removed down to bare wood, repaint. Because latex paint breathes, or permits moisture to pass through the paint film more readily than alkyd paint does, always use a quality acrylic latex paint on peeling or problem exterior trim. Apply a coat of exterior latex trim paint, and when the base coat is dry, apply a final finish coat.

Skylights

Skylights can create two potential water problems; the first is that the window penetrates the roof deck, thus creating a potential roof leak if installation is not carefully done.

The second problem is that skylights position a window pane at the highest point in the room, so that the pane is more susceptible to fogging or frosting due to the effects of rising moisture-laden air. This condensed moisture will eventually rain down to the floor or furnishings below or may frost over the window pane.

To avoid these skylight problems, purchase the best quality skylight you can afford. Visit dealers who sell quality products, carefully compare the specifications of each unit, and buy the best.

Second, be sure that the manufacturer's directions are strictly followed during skylight installation. This is not a do-it-yourself project: after selecting the unit, ask the dealer to recommend a qualified installer. In areas of high annual snowfall, it is best to frame a wooden base support or riser around the roof opening, then mount the skylight atop the riser. This procedure will raise the skylight above the potential winter snow level, and will help achieve a leak-proof installation. (See "Curb-Mounted Fixed Skylight" illustration on page 94.) Most manufacturers provide proper flashing to water-proof the joint between the skylight and the roof.

Double-Hung Windows

If you have older double-hung windows, moisture can pass through the holes in the side frames that hold the sash cords and pulleys. To remedy this situation, there are two options.

The first is to remove the sash cord and weights. The best way to do this is to remove the interior window trim and pull out the cords, weights, and pulleys. Then use kraft- or aluminum-faced batt insulation to fill and insulate the weight cavities. Position the insulation so the aluminum-faced side is to the inside, toward the living area. Plug the cord holes in the side frames and replace the trim. To ensure operation of the windows, install spring clips on the frame to exert tension against the window sash and hold the window sash in the open position. Note that these springs may not provide enough tension on very large or heavy window sashes.

The second option is to install a special plastic cover over the holes that will allow the window to operate. Buy these cover devices at your home center.

Coping with Skylight Problems

If you already have problems with leaks on a skylight, have the installer or a roofer inspect and repair the unit.

If the leak is between the skylight and the roof, a roofer may be able to improve the flashing and seal to eliminate the leak. If the leak is through the skylight structure, the only permanent solution may be to replace the unit with one of better quality.

By dehumidifying and following the humidity-reduction steps suggested in Chapter 6, Humidity Problems, you may be able to reduce interior humidity levels and thus limit the formation of condensation or frost on the window. For example, when cooking a large meal, or when you see condensation on the skylight pane, open the unit and permit the excess moisture to exit.

Window Replacement

Besides energy savings from better thermal and air infiltration control, window replacement will provide other benefits: reduced drafts will improve occupant comfort and new windows can transform a house. If your windows are drafty, peeling, damaged, or decayed, consider replacing them.

New wood window models may have aluminum- or vinyl-clad exterior trim. This permanent exterior cladding will not peel or rot and will reduce painting and other window maintenance. To take advantage of these features, consider buying replacement windows with no-maintenance exterior trim cladding.

As in the selection of any expensive components, there is no substitute for quality in windows. A wise business adage says that quality and good design will be remembered long after the price is forgotten.

DOORS

Like windows, exterior doors can suffer from moisture problems, and for many of the same reasons. Moisture can penetrate between the rough opening and the door frame, causing wood decay or peeling paint on exterior trim.

Wood Doors

Wood doors offer time-proven durability and the warm look of wood, but if they are not properly protected from moisture and weather, they are subject to shrinkage, cracking, and warping. These problems are often due to moisture entering the wood. To prevent sticking in the frame, door edges are left unpainted, and moisture can enter the door through these unsealed edges. If you have a wood door, remove the door and apply a clear wood sealer to all edges. This will reduce moisture penetration through all parts of the door.

Ill-fitting or worn weather-stripping can allow air and moisture to penetrate through the cracks between the door and the frame. You may be surprised to learn just how much moisture, air, and dust can penetrate the door opening.

Consider that to permit the door to open there is a perimeter crack around the door that is 20 feet (6 meters) long and ⅛ inch (0.3 centimeters) wide. The total area of this crack is equal to a hole that is 2-½ inches (6 centimeters) by 12 inches (20 centimeters) or about the same size—and effect—as having a hole the size of a brick in your wall. If it has been years since you have replaced your door weather-stripping, see the energy-efficient materials available at your home center store. Each kit contains enough weather-stripping to do an exterior door, including any nails or brads that are necessary for installation. Check before each heating season; replace when worn or torn.

Often overlooked is the door sweep, the weather-stripping that seals the crack between the bottom of the door and the threshold. It is usually attached to the door with three or four small screws. Modern door sweeps may have multiple layers of vinyl that ensure a tight seal at the door threshold. This

weatherstrip not only blocks infiltration of air and moisture but also is a barrier to dust and insects. Examine your door sweep at the beginning of each heating season, and replace any door sweep that is ill-fitting, old, or worn.

Clear Finishes for Wood Doors

A tough exterior paint coat may be the best protective finish for an exterior door, but many people prefer a natural wood appearance protected with a clear finish of polyurethane or varnish. However, ordinary clear exterior varnishes are subject to ultraviolet degradation from the sun, and may become dull and faded through simple exposure.

If you have problems with a clear finish on your exterior doors, remove the old finish, using a dust mask and eye protection. If moisture has left black stains on the door, use oxalic acid, available in crystal form at paint stores, to remove the stains. When stains are removed, clean and sand the bare wood. For the new finish, select a tough, water-resistant coating such as spar or marine varnish, or choose one of the new exterior polyurethane finishes that contain an ultraviolet blocker that resists damage from sunlight. Apply either of these finishes according to

Stanley Entry Door

New-age door has the look of wood but is actually wood-grained fiberglass. A polyurethane core makes the door energy efficient; a compression weatherstrip, adjustable threshold, and thermal threshold break seal against air and moisture entry.

the manufacturer's directions: most recommend at least two coats of finish on exterior surfaces. If you wait until the finish has deteriorated, refinishing the door will be a large job, so depending on your weather, it may be best to renew these clear finishes on an annual basis. For the best results, refinish the door in the fall, just before severe winter weather begins. If you live in a hot climate the best time to refinish is in the spring, before summer starts.

Warped Wood Doors

If a wood door is not properly sealed on all faces and edges, moisture may enter the wood and cause the door to warp. Fortunately, this warping can often be reversed.

If a door is warped, wait until dry weather, then remove the door from its hinges and remove any peeling or failing finish. Use oxalic acid to bleach any stains.

Place the door, convex or curved side up, over a pair of sawhorses set near each end of the door. Now place heavy weights, such as two concrete blocks, on the center area of the door. Leave the weights in place for several days, checking each day to see whether the door has become straighter. When the warp or curve of the door is gone and the door is flat,

Patio Door

New-generation patio doors have energy-efficient glass, improved weatherstrip, and no-maintenance exteriors.

apply a coat of clear sealer to all the edges of the door. Then refinish the door as desired, with two coats of paint or polyurethane finish on each face of the door. Tip: Painters often apply an extra coat of finish to the convex side of a warped door. Paint tension from the extra coat may help relieve the warp and straighten the door.

Insulated Doors

Due to the increased interest in energy conservation, new energy-efficient insulated doors have become very popular. These doors have a core of foam insulation, and may be clad on the faces either with steel or fiberglass.

Insulated doors do not warp, crack, or swell in damp weather. They are factory fitted with magnetic weather-stripping that ensures an airtight seal between the door and the door frame. These insulated doors provide as high an R-value as door/storm door combinations.

The factory finish reduces maintenance on insulated doors. Some of these steel and fiberglass doors are embossed so the finish resembles a wood grain. By using stains and a wood-graining tool available at most paint stores, you can finish any insulated door with a wood-grain pattern.

Patio Doors

Through improved technology and extensive testing, manufacturers have improved the thermal efficiency of both metal and wood patio doors. Metal patio doors have split frames with insulation between the frames, but metal patio doors still conduct cold, and although the metal doors have improved thermal efficiency, I advise having a quality wood patio door in cold climates. If you will be buying a new patio door, check the new model homes or open houses offered by builders in your area. You will be able to determine which type of patio door—wood or metal—is commonly used in your climate. Patio doors have double or insulating glass panes. Over time, a leak may develop in the seal between the insulating panes, which will allow moisture to enter the space, condense, and cloud the door glass. There is no solution for this problem; you must replace the glass pane.

Because of their large glass pane area, doors are prone to condensed moisture or frost on the interior side of the glass in cold weather. If the door frame is metal, the frame may also become covered with frost, sometimes to the point that it is impossible to open the door.

If the forced-air heating system is properly engineered, there will be a hot air vent in the floor in front of the patio door. Always keep this vent open, and if possible adjust it to direct the air flow toward the door. The heated air from this vent will rise and sweep over the door glass, warming the glass and removing condensation.

If you have this type of floor-mounted heat duct in front of the patio door, and are still getting condensation or frost on the door glass or frame, lower the humidity level in the house. For a review of suggested remedies, see Chapter 6, Humidity Problems.

If you have lowered indoor humidity to your basic comfort level, and there is still condensation on the patio door, open the door briefly every few hours to allow excess moisture to escape. Set a small fan near the closed patio door, and aim the fan so the air stream flows over the glass. This precaution will both raise the temperature of the glass and will carry away moisture that reaches the door.

If there are black water stains on the door, remove the finish and use oxalic acid to bleach the stains. Then refinish the door, using a durable interior paint, marine varnish, or polyurethane finish.

Garage Doors

Garage doors are available in wood, hardboard, steel, or fiberglass. Insulated garage doors are available, but when choosing a door remember that insulation is useful only as a thermal barrier between heated and unheated areas. There is no energy advantage in having an insulated door in an unheated or detached garage.

Steel and fiberglass garage doors are resistant to moisture attack, but wood and hardboard doors may suffer several kinds of moisture damage. At the factory, the garage door weather-stripping is often nailed to the unsealed lower edge of the bottom door panel. With a hard rain or snow accumulation, water may reach the bottom of the door, and the water will wick up through the wood or hardboard in the bottom door panel. This can cause warping, staining, paint peeling, or decay in the door panel.

Pry away the rubber or vinyl weather-stripping at the bottom of the door, and inspect the bottom edge to see if it is painted or sealed. If it is not, remove the weather-stripping and apply a coat of latex paint or sealer to the unsealed edge of the wood or hardboard. This will provide a barrier to water entry at the door bottom. Replace the weather-stripping.

Because of rain or roof water splashing onto the garage apron or drive, the paint finish on the lower section of the garage door often will weather more quickly than the paint on upper panels. This is also true of the lower courses of siding on the garage and house. Inspect the lower panels of the garage door frequently, and refinish them when you see any indication of peeling paint, water stains, or mildew on the door. Pressure-wash the house siding and garage door at least once per year to remove grime and dirt that will support moisture buildup and mildew growth.

Attic Access Doors

Ceiling-mounted attic access doors interrupt the ceiling vapor retarder and the attic insulation blanket. If you have a one-piece hinged or lift-up attic door, paint the room side of the door with alkyd paint to provide some protection against moisture passage. Cut foam insulation such as Styrofoam to fit the door, and use an adhesive to attach the foam insulation to the attic side of the door. If you have a pull-down or folding-ladder type attic door, cut a panel of foam insulation large enough to overlap the framing around the attic door. Push the insulation panel aside when you need access to the attic; when you exit the attic, pull the foam insulation panel in place so it overlaps the entire opening.

PART III

WATER IN YOUR HOME

CHAPTER 8

Plumbing and Moisture

To control water-related problems you must first eliminate all sources of unwanted moisture. Plumbing problems such as leaking faucets, water sumps that are not covered, and moisture condensation on the toilet bowl or hot or cold water pipes can all contribute to excess moisture. To eliminate all moisture sources, take an inspection tour of your entire plumbing system and make the suggested repairs.

LEAKING FAUCETS

Water that leaks either from around the faucet body or through the faucet spout can contribute to indoor humidity from evaporation, and moisture condensation that drips on floors or cabinet bases can cause damage such as wood rot or decay to flooring or cabinets. Moisture that accumulates under a sink can also provide an inviting environment for household insects such as roaches, which will flourish wherever there is moisture, warmth, and food. Check around the sink at faucet bases for signs of leakage. Also check the faucets to be sure they shut off completely and do not leak from the spout. If leaks are evident around either the base or the spout of the faucet, do not crank on the faucet handle to force it to close. Applying too much pressure on a faucet handle can distort the faucet body and ruin the faucet. Instead, repair the faucet to ensure it is leak-free.

There are a variety of faucet types, and it is likely that there are several different types in your home. Faucet types include stem or compression faucets, often found at tub or exterior bib faucets; ball-type faucets, cartridge faucets, and disc-type faucets, usually found in bath vanity sinks or in

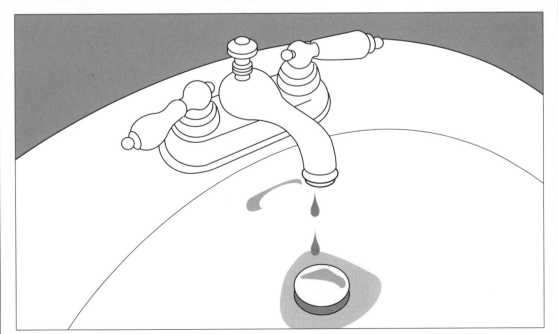

Leaking Faucet

Leaking faucets waste water, stain fixtures, and add humidity to the house.

Evaporation

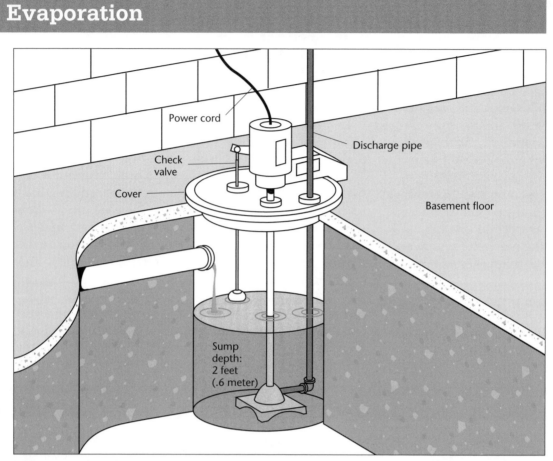

Power cord

Discharge pipe

Check valve

Cover

Basement floor

Sump depth: 2 feet (.6 meter)

Sump pump is shown here with cover in place. Open sumps, toilets, or any standing water can add humidity to the house.

kitchen sinks. Determine what type of faucet you have, and repair as indicated. If you cannot determine which type of faucet you need to repair, take the manufacturer's name from the faucet and ask your dealer to advise which faucet repair kit you need.

CLOTHES WASHER HOSES

Hot and cold water faucets near the clothes washer sup-

ply water to the washer via rubber hoses. Leaving these faucets turned on when the washer is not in use means there is always water pressure in the supply hoses, and the hoses will be subject to the same pressure and potential leakage as water pipes. These rubber water hoses were never intended to be constantly kept under water pressure, and should be turned on when water is needed at the washer, then turned off when the laundry

is done. Many homeowners have come home from a trip to find that during their absence the water hoses on the washer burst, flooding the basement or laundry room. If your water hoses are leaking, or there is a soft or spongy feeling when you squeeze the hoses, replace the hoses before they fail. Replacement hoses are available at most appliance or plumbing supply stores.

Replacing Toilet Wax Ring

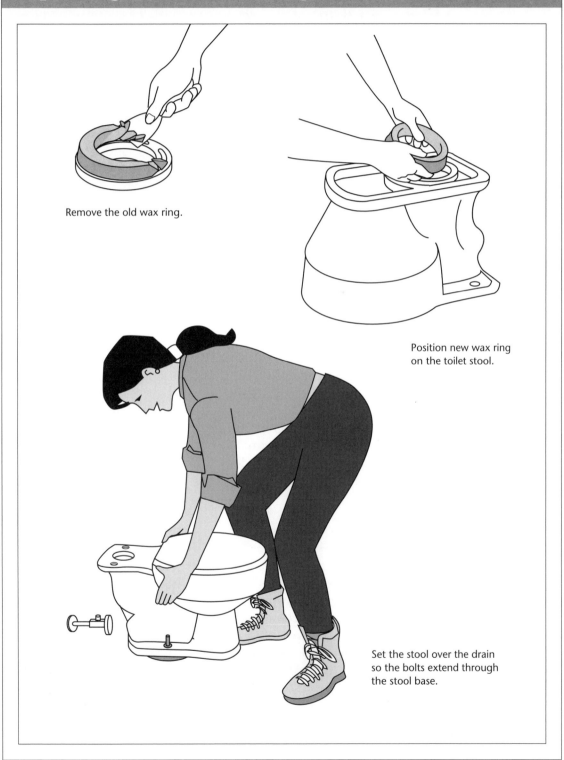

Remove the old wax ring.

Position new wax ring on the toilet stool.

Set the stool over the drain so the bolts extend through the stool base.

MOISTURE FROM EVAPORATION

Because moisture in any form will seek equilibrium with the ambient air, standing water will evaporate more readily in a climate of low humidity than in a high humidity area. To help control indoor humidity, attempt to block all sources of moisture evaporation, especially of standing water in toilets, sumps, or drains.

Toilets and Sumps

If high indoor humidity is a problem, always keep the toilet lid closed to minimize evaporation from the toilet bowl. Likewise, if you have a sump system that collects wastewater or water runoff from drainage tiles, cover the sump to minimize evaporation. Most sumps come complete with a hardboard or plastic cover, but they are often lost or misplaced. You can buy a replacement at plumbing shops or from your home center, or make your own from tempered hardboard.

Condensation on Fixtures

When a toilet is flushed, the standing water in the toilet bowl is flushed down the drain, and the toilet tank and bowl refill with cold water. This incoming cold water will cool the fixture, and if the bathroom is warm or humidity is high, the airborne moisture will condense on the toilet tank or bowl.

After condensing, the water will drip down the fixture, onto the floor, and under the toilet to wet the wood subfloor or underlayment. In houses more than 40 years old the subfloor may be 1 inch × 8 inch (2.5 centimeters × 20 centimeters) boards, which warp when wet. In modern houses, the subfloor is plywood. The moisture then can attack the adhesive that holds the wood plies together, causing the plywood to delaminate and develop bulges under the floor covering or loosen it. The only remedy is to remove the existing floor covering and replace it. If the wetted subfloor has also decayed, it is essential to tear up the existing floor and replace the damaged subfloor, then install new floor covering.

There are three steps that can be taken to stop condensation on a toilet fixture. The first is to buy a terrycloth cover for the toilet tank. These covers warm the tank and toilet bowl to reduce condensation; the terrycloth or toweling absorbs any moisture that does condense on the fixture and prevents the moisture from dripping onto the floor.

Another cure for moisture condensation is to install a Styrofoam insulation kit inside the toilet tank. To install the insulation, shut off the water supply valve underneath the toilet tank, flush the toilet to remove the water from the tank, then use a towel to wipe and dry the inside of the toilet tank. Apply an adhesive to the inside surfaces of the tank, and install the styrofoam insulation kit inside the tank. The added mass will also reduce water usage.

A third method to eliminate condensation is to have a plumber install a mixing valve to supply warm water to the toilet fixture. Rather than drawing water for the toilet from the cold water supply, a mixing valve will draw in and mix cold and hot water so that the water will be warm when it fills the fixture. Because the fixture is no longer cold, condensation will not form on it.

Toilet Wax Ring

Water accumulation around the base of the toilet stool may come from condensation; however, if no condensation is visible on the toilet fixture the source may be a leaking wax ring or seal between the toilet base and the drain pipe. If the problem is not corrected, the seeping water will wet and rot the subfloor or cause a bond failure between the subfloor or underlayment and the finished floor covering.

First mop up any water from the floor so you can follow the seeping water to its source. If the water reappears on the floor and seems to be coming from under the base, the problem is a faulty wax ring. The wax ring is a doughnut-shaped device that seals the joint between the drain pipe and the toilet base.

If you determine that the water source is a leaking wax ring, turn off the water supply valve, located under the toilet tank. Then flush the toilet twice: the first flush will empty the toilet tank and the second flush will drain the water from the toilet bowl. There will be no water in the bowl to leak until the water to the fixture is turned on again.

To remove the toilet tank from the base, remove the nuts from the two hold-down bolts at the bottom of the tank, under the toilet bowl.

Next, remove the nuts from the two hold-down bolts at the bottom of the toilet bowl, at floor level. Carefully lift the bowl away and turn it over a pail to catch any water remaining in the U-trap of the stool. Remove the old wax ring, clean the area, and install the new ring by pressing it into the base, being sure to center the ring over the drain hole. Then set the base over the two hold-down bolts and rock the bowl side-to-side to seat the ring. Replace and tighten the nuts on the bolts, replace the tank over the toilet bowl, and secure it in place with the two bolts that connect the two units. To test for leaks, turn the water back on and flush the toilet. Caution: do not caulk the crack between the toilet base and the floor. Caulk at this point will seal any leaking water under the base, and may rot the floor before you are aware of a leak.

Condensation on Water Pipes

At locations where cold water pipes pass through a humid area such as a basement or a laundry room, condensation often occurs on the cold pipe surfaces. Conversely, during cold winters, cool, damp basement air may condense on hot water pipes. To prevent condensation on water pipes, buy pipe insulation at a home center, and insulate both cold and hot water pipes.

One type of pipe insulation is available in foil-faced rolls of fiberglass, which are simply wound around the pipe and secured in place with duct tape. This insulation is useful where the pipes are not a straight run.

A second type of pipe insulation is tubular foam plastic. The foam insulation is available in lengths of 4 feet (1.3 meters), and with a variety of hole diameters to fit any household water pipe diameter. The foam tubes are split down the side and are slipped over the pipes. To ensure that the insulation is not interrupted, fit the ends of the foam insulation tube together carefully, and use duct tape to hold the insulation in place.

Tubular foam insulation is the best choice when you are trying to insulate pipes in close quarters, where there is no working room to wrap the insulation batts around the pipes, such as when insulating a water pipe that runs from the basement up into a wall cavity. In this case the insulation can be fitted over the pipe at the lower end and slipped upward into position in the restricted area.

PLUGGED PLUMBING DRAINS

Of all plumbing problems, the most frustrating and damaging may be a plugged drain. To minimize the danger of drain backup and flooding in the sink or basement, follow these preventive maintenance tips.

To prevent plugged drains, first avoid putting

potential plug materials into the drains. Use plastic drain strainers, available at any home center, in the kitchen and lavatory sinks and the bathtub drain.

To eliminate plugs from lint in laundry tub drains, slip a mesh-type strainer onto the water discharge hose of the clothes washer. To ensure its efficiency, replace the strainer frequently.

When cleaning up after a do-it-yourself project, do not flush repair materials down the drain. Materials such as patch plaster, wallboard cement, and concrete patchers are soft and pliable when flushed down the drain, but will set up or harden in the drain pipes and create a drain plug that will be difficult to remove. Instead, mix patching products in disposable paper containers, available at paint stores, and let the leftover patchers harden in the containers. Then dispose of the container and waste in the trash receptacle. Or, mix repair materials in a plastic pail and let leftovers harden in the pail. After the material has hardened, flex the sides of the plastic pail to pop out the hardened materials. Dispose of the hardened materials in the trash.

Garbage disposal frequently cause blockages. To ensure plug-free drains, run water in the sink until you are sure you have flushed all the food waste completely out of the small-diameter sink drain pipe and into the larger main sewer pipe. Neglecting this flushing period can permit food particles to accumulate and plug the small-diameter sink drain pipe.

The chief cause of plugged bathroom drains is the accumulation of soap particles or human hair in drain pipes. When a bar of soap is reduced to a sliver, dispose of it in the bathroom wastebasket. Do not continue to use the soap until it breaks into small fragments that can plug the drain.

Human hair does not deteriorate from moisture exposure, so when hair enters a drain it often will cling to the walls of the drain pipe. To reduce hair accumulation in the shower or sink, comb or brush your hair before you shampoo, then deposit the hair in the wastebasket. To catch falling hair while shampooing, place a plastic strainer over the tub drain.

Be sure to dispose of all paper products in the wastebasket. Toilet paper is made to degrade when wet, but other paper products are not.

Drain Maintence

When the main sewer drain plugs up and floods the house or basement floor, the result is a nightmare. Do not wait until a sewer backup occurs to have your main sewer pipes cleaned. Instead, consider sewer cleaning to be preventive maintenance.

Tiny tree roots seek moisture in the earth, so they often grow into the joints between main sewer drain pipes. If there is a tree sitting over or near the sewer drain, have the drain cleaned by professionals to check for root buildup in the pipes. Tree roots can plug the pipes and cause a sewer backup, as well as growing so large that they will crack and collapse the drain pipes. The remedy then involves excavating a trench to the street sewer pipe and installing new sewer pipes. This is an expensive project that can easily be avoided by keeping the sewer drain clear.

The frequency of sewer cleaning maintenance depends on the number of people living in the house and other factors such as the proximity of trees to your drains. Ask your sewer serviceperson to suggest how often you should have sewer drain pipes cleaned.

To inspect for sewer blockage, some city works departments will run small TV cameras down street sewer mains and advise homeowners of potential problems. To avoid the mess and damage of a flooded basement or bathroom floor,

Cleaning the Main Drain

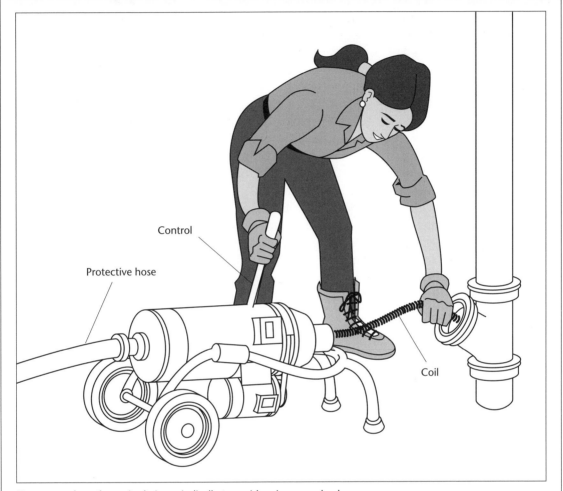

Have a pro clean the main drain periodically to avoid major sewer backup.

heed their advice and set up a regular drain cleaning schedule. Contact your city utilities department to see if this service is available.

BATHTUB AND SHOWER LEAKS

Water can cause serious damage behind a wall if it leaks through a crack between ceramic tiles, or through the joint where tub and ceramic tile meet. The water may cause wood decay, or may soak or wick up through the tile substrate and cause a complete failure of the tile job.

To prevent future water damage to tiled surfaces, when building new or remodeling, provide a concrete base for the ceramic tile installation. A concrete tile base will not soak up water and loosen tile. Ordinary wallboard or plaster can soak or wick up water from the crack between the tub and tile. This water may penetrate upward from the tub/tile juncture for a distance of 1 foot (0.3 meters) or more. When subjected to continuously wet conditions, the plaster or plaster core in wallboard will deteriorate to a soft, pulpy mass. When this happens, the plaster will soften and no longer have the strength to support the tiles, which fall off. At this point the only remedy is completely tearing out the old tile and walls and building anew—a large and expensive job. To prevent future water damage to a new bathroom, have the tile setter use wire lath and concrete to build a concrete base or substrate for the tile. Another option is to use wallboard screws to secure reinforced concrete panels such as Durock™ onto the stud wall, as a base for installing the tile.

Water can penetrate between the ceramic tile and the substrate through neglected grout joints between the tiles. Inspect the tiled areas carefully for cracks or deteriorating grout. Regrout the tiles to seal the grout joints and ensure a waterproof tile barrier. Use a grout saw to clean the old grout from the joints between tiles, then use a sponge or rubber squeegee to apply the grout over the entire tile surface. By using the squeegee you will leave grout between the tile joints, and can wipe excess grout away from the tile surfaces. Because grout becomes brittle when dry, do not use grout to seal the joint where the tub and tile meet (see below).

When the grout is slightly set, use a damp sponge to clean the grout residue from the face of the tile. To clean and shine the tiles, use clean towels to wipe the remaining dull haze from the tile surface when it is dry.

The most common crack in tile, and the crack at which water entry is most damaging, is at the point where the tub and tile meet. The tub will settle when the tub is filled with the combined weight of the bath water and the bather. This will cause a crack to open between the lip of the tub and the wall tile. To prevent this, use a caulk that will not harden, but will continue to stretch a bit after curing. Shop for tub/tile caulks at any home center or paint store.

To apply a tub/tile caulk, first clean any old caulk from the cracks between the tub and tile. Remove any debris, then clean the area with rubbing alcohol to remove any residual soap scum. Then apply the new tub/tile caulk to the crack, being sure to completely fill the crack. Use a wet forefinger to smooth and level the caulk. Let the grout and caulk cure as per label directions before exposing to water.

As extra insurance against water entry behind tile, after bathing and drying yourself use the bath towel to wipe water from the tile surface. As you dry the tile, inspect the tiled surface for cracks. To control bathroom humidity, remove damp towels and bath mats from the bathroom when you have finished, and deposit them in the clothes washer.

Bathtub Leak

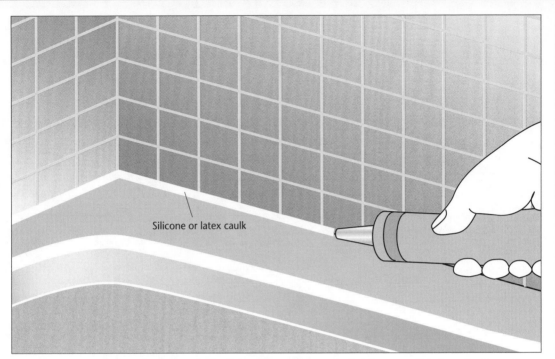

Silicone or latex caulk

A common source of water damage to tiled walls is water entry through tile joints or at tile/tub cracks. Grout tile joints often and use a flexible silicone or latex caulk to seal the joint between the tile and tub.

CHAPTER 9

Water Conservation

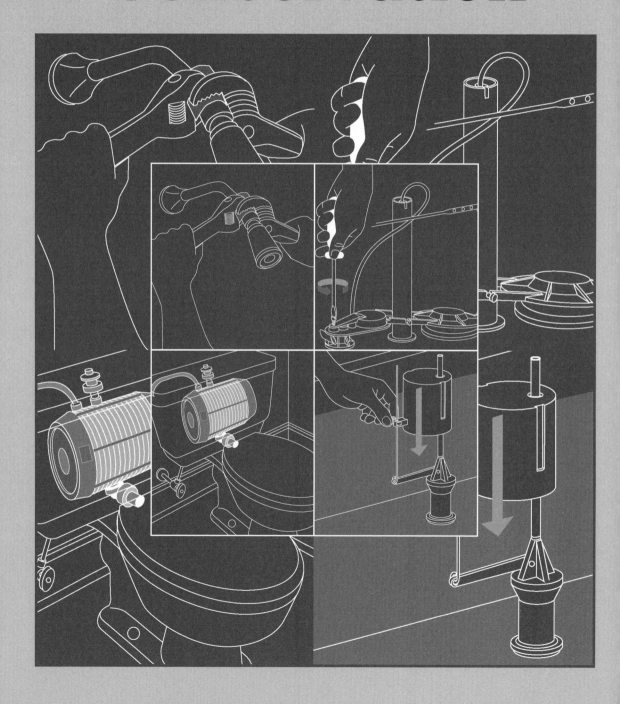

With the growth in agricultural activity, industry, and population, water consumption has increased dramatically. In states with a huge population and a large agribusiness, such as California, and in high-growth desert states such as Arizona, the demand for water threatens to overwhelm supply. In California it is estimated that 85 percent of the state's water is used for agricultural irrigation. In the San Joaquin Valley, a major agricultural area, pumping subterranean water for irrigation purposes began in 1925. Since that time, the floor of the valley has sunk 10 feet (3 meters) as the water has been pumped from beneath it.

In New York City an estimated 20 percent of all city water is wasted through leaks in antiquated water mains. Many predict that the next major resource crisis may be the shortage of water, not oil. Water rationing has already become commonplace in many cities; through stringent conservation measures the city of San Francisco has cut water consumption by 25 percent. In this chapter we will review ways to cut your family's water consumption by 50 percent or more.

PER CAPITA WATER CONSUMPTION

On a per capita basis, the U.S. consumes 80 gallons (320 liters) of water per day, and it is estimated that 62 percent of that water, or 50 gallons (189 liters) of water per person, is wasted. For example, per capita outdoor water usage for lawn and garden accounts for 28 gallons (112 liters) of water

Shower

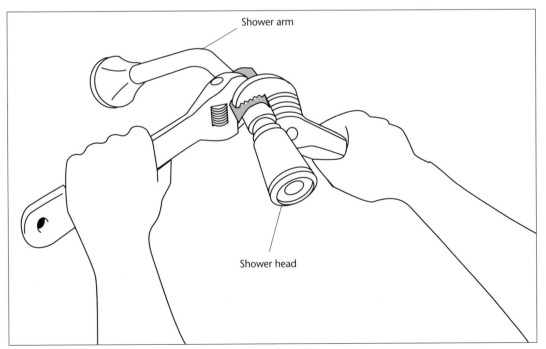

Install low-flow shower heads to conserve bath water.

Toilet

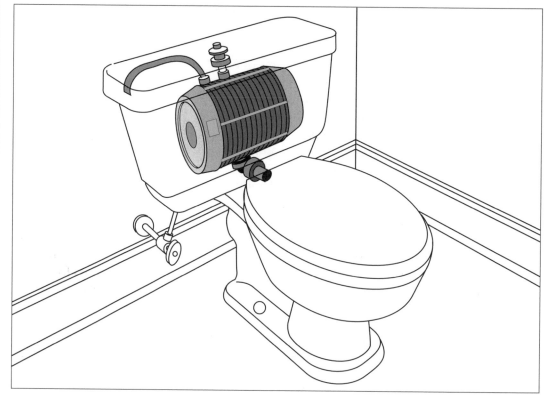

New toilets use about one-third as much water as older units. This unit uses air power to increase flush velocity.

daily; toilet use, 17 gallons (68 liters); bathing, 13 gallons (52 liters); and laundry, 11 gallons (44 liters).

To reduce water consumption, we can change wasteful habits, repair leaking faucets and pipes, replace or repair plumbing fixtures, and control water usage for purposes such as watering the lawn or washing the car.

REDUCING WATER CONSUMPTION

Lingering in the shower, letting water run while brushing our teeth or washing our hair, using the toilet as a disposal to flush away paper waste, rinsing garden vegetables under running water, overwatering the lawn and garden, and hose washing the car all can consume a large amount of water. However, with little effort, we could eliminate much of the waste.

To reduce household water usage, install low-flow shower heads and limit time in the shower. Shut water off while you are brushing your teeth, and wash all items in a stoppered sink rather than under running water.

Water generated by an air conditioner or a dehumidifier is mineral-free, and if it is poured down the drain, the clean water becomes so much sewage to be treated.

Rather than pouring it down the drain, collect and use the water for household purposes. Rather than buying distilled water, use the water in your steam iron, or to water the garden or houseplants. Minerals in

Float Ball

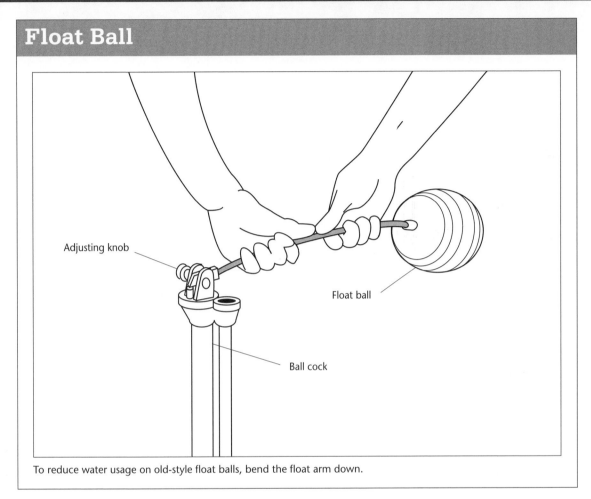

Adjusting knob

Float ball

Ball cock

To reduce water usage on old-style float balls, bend the float arm down.

water also can affect the color quality of latex paints: use the mineral-free water for thinning latex paints and for paint tool cleanup. Because mineral-free water will not corrode the radiator, mix it 50:50 with antifreeze and use it in the radiator of the car.

When washing the car at home, first use the hose to rinse the car with clean water and remove the grit and grime from the car finish. Then wash the car with a pail and sponge to remove dirt. Finally, use the hose to rinse the car. When possible, drive your car through an automated car wash, which is more efficient and uses less water, rather than washing it at home.

PLUMBING

Leaking Faucets

To conserve water, repair leaking pipes or faucets. A leak of one drop per second can waste 2,300 gallons (9,500 liters) of water per year. Multiply this figure by the number of leaking faucets in the house, and you may find that repairing the faucets will result in considerable water—and cost—savings.

Plumbing Fixtures

Old-style plumbing fixtures each waste hundreds of gallons (liters) of water per year. For example, older toilets may use up to 7 gallons (28 liters) of water per flush; low-flow toilets may operate on 1-½ gallons (6 liters) per flush. If you are not ready to

Float Cup

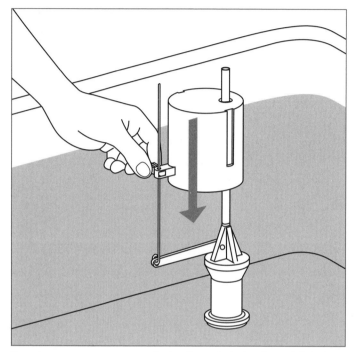

To reduce water usage on new flush valves, pinch the clip and slide the cup down the rod.

Shower heads

Old-style shower heads, with a water flow rate of 5 to 8 gallons (20 to 32 liters) per minute, waste thousands of gallons—or liters—of water daily. New low-flow shower heads use only 3 gallons (12 liters) of water or less per minute. This means that a low-flow shower head can save 10 gallons (40 liters) of water or more during each three-minute shower. For a family of four, that could be a savings of 40 gallons (160 liters) per day × 365 days = 14,600 gallons (58,000 liters) of water saved per year.

Laundry

To conserve water, wash only full loads of clothes and select the wash cycle carefully. Using the permanent press cycle may require an extra rinse, which means you are using an extra water fill. That extra fill can use 5 gallons (20 liters) of water. To save energy, use cold-water detergents and run the washer on the cold temperature setting only.

Dishwashing

Hand washing dishes under running water can use 5 gallons (20 liters) of water per minute.

If you hand wash dishes, do not leave the water running. Put the stopper in the drain and fill the sink with hot water. Wash the dishes,

replace the toilet fixture, you can bend the float ball arm down so the toilet tank shuts off before extra water is used to fill it. Or fill plastic bottles with water and place them in the toilet tank to displace a gallon or more of the water. This permits the toilet to flush, and does not affect toilet operation, but does reduce water consumption. At repair time, replace the old flush-ball type with a modern plastic flush valve. The plastic flush valves are adjustable so you can set them to shut off when the water level in the toilet tank reaches a preselected depth.

To calculate the water savings of low-flow toilets, consider that, when compared to older units, the toilet saves about 4 gallons (16 liters) of water per flush. Let us assume that for a family of four the toilet will be flushed an average of 16 times per day, an estimate that may be conservative. Multiply 4 gallons (16 liters) of water saved per flush × 16 flushes = 64 gallons (256 liters of water saved per day × 365 days = 23,360 gallons (93,440 liters) of water saved per year per household by installing a low-flush toilet.

Metered Valve

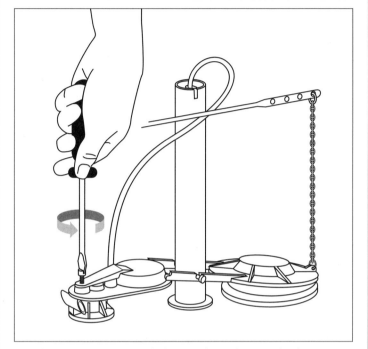

Turn the screwdriver counterclockwise to lower the water level.

then place them in the dish rack. When you are finished washing dishes, use the spray nozzle to rinse the dishes.

Compared to hand washing, using the dishwasher can save up to 10 gallons (40 liters) of water. For maximum savings, run only full loads when you wash dishes.

LAWN AND GARDEN

Outside water usage is the largest single category of all home water consumption, using up to 28 gallons (112 liters) of water per day per person. Most of this water goes on the lawn and garden. By adopting good conservation methods, you can greatly reduce the amount of water used for these purposes and, at the same time, have a healthier lawn.

Test the Soil's pH Balance

Soil that has a proper pH balance will grow a healthy lawn and require less water and chemicals. The term "pH" refers to potential hydrogen. The right pH balance for your lawn will vary by climate and type of turf. Check with your local garden center or college agricultural offices to learn the right pH for your lawn.

For most lawns experts advise having a neutral pH of between 5 and 7. This means that the soil is neither acid nor alkaline. Experts recommend adding lime to neutralize acid soil, and adding sulphur to balance alkaline soil.

If soil is compacted, aerate the lawn. The aerator machine will punch hundreds of small holes in the lawn so that moisture and nutrients reach the roots more easily.

One clue that the lawn is getting too little water is thatch buildup, which is caused by grass roots growing to the surface to seek water. Night crawlers (large worms that are active at night) are evidence of thatch buildup. Do not use chemicals to rid the lawn of night crawlers; rent a dethatcher, a sort of power rake, instead.

When you water the lawn, apply at least the equivalent of 1 inch (2.5 centimeters) of rain with each watering, which is enough water to penetrate to root level. Water requirements vary by grass species and by your climate. As a general rule, experts advise that bluegrass lawns require a total of 2 inches (5 centimeters) of water every two weeks. That total includes

Lawn Sprinkler System

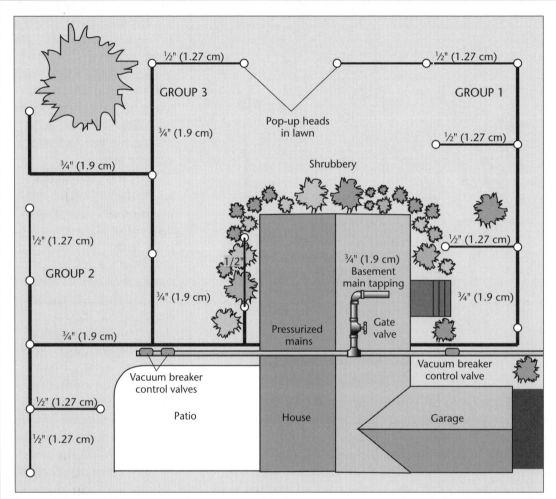

Automatic lawn sprinkler system permits you to control and conserve on water usage. Two inches (5 centimeters) of water per two-week period (including rain) keeps lawn healthy without wasting water.

both rainfall and watering or irrigation. If you have a healthy lawn, a 2-inch (5 centimeters) total of rainfall in two weeks is sufficient to maintain the lawn, and you will not have to water to supplement the rain.

To ensure you don't overwater the lawn, measure the amount of water that falls from your sprinkler.

Set a wide-mouth container such as a coffee can in the path of the sprinkler. Paint marks levels at 1-inch (2.5-centimeters) and 2-inch (5-centimeters) depths inside the can. When you have applied a sufficient amount of water, move the sprinkler to the next area.

Automatic sprinkler systems can be adjusted

to deliver a preset amount lof water to the lawn. Unfortunately, unless the system is monitored, the sprinkler may be running during a downpour of rain, an obvious waste of water. Monitor and manage the lawn sprinkler system so lthat the lawn receives a total of 2 inches (5 centimeters) of water, including both rain and watering, every two weeks.

When you have finished watering the lawn, wait 12 hours and then push a screwdriver blade into the turf. If the blade penetrates easily to a depth of 5 or 6 inches (12.5 to 15 centimeters), you can be sure that you have watered enough to reach the root structure of the grass.

Mowing the Lawn

To prevent grass from wilting and to retard the rate of moisture evaporation from the lawn, always let the grass grow to a height of 3 inches (7.5 centimeters) , then mow to a height of 2 inches (5 centimeters). Keeping the grass at least 2 inches (5 centimeters) long will help block out weeds, shade the soil, and prevent moisture evaporation from the lawn. Tall grass also means deep roots, and forcing roots to reach deep for moisture will help make the grass more resistant to summer drought.

Do not bag and dispose of grass clippings. Leave the grass clippings on the lawn: the clippings comprise about 85 percent water, and will return both moisture and valuable nutrients to the soil. The John Deere Company estimates that leaving the grass clippings on the lawn after each mowing provides nutrients equal to one feeding of fertilizer per season.

Drought-resistant Grass Seed

When you mow a lawn, the grass never sets seed, so occasional overseeding is necessary to ensure a thick turf. When reseeding, choose hardy grasses, such as tall fescues, zoysia grass, Bermuda grass, and St. Augustine grass, which require less moisture and are more drought resistant.

Consult with your local garden center to find a grass variety that will flourish in your climate while consuming a minimum of water.

Mulches

Mulches are organic or inorganic materials that can moderate soil temperatures, limit weed growth, and reduce moisture evaporation. Use mulch in flower or vegetable gardens, and to cover areas under trees, shrubs, and plants.

Mulches also can conserve moisture while being decorative and retarding weed growth. Cedar chips, cedar or redwood bark, peat moss, and decorative stones are among the many mulch choices. Also check with your city or parks department; many cities offer free mulch that has been processed during tree removal or maintenance. Or, use a chipper-shredder to convert yard waste such as storm-blown or pruned tree limbs to organic mulch.

CHAPTER 10

Floods

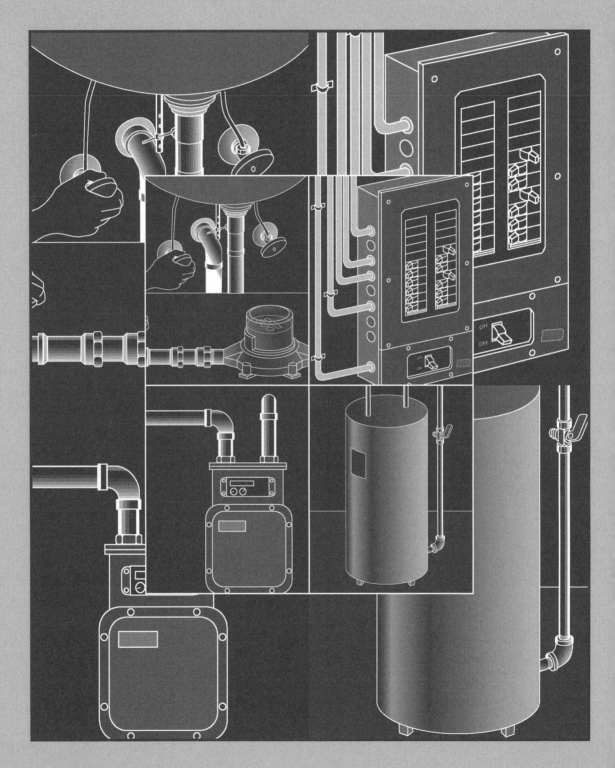

The ultimate threat involving water damage to your house is a flood. During the extreme weather of the past few years, much of the United States has been subjected to record flooding; the danger of flooding is exacerbated if the house is near a stream, river, or drainage pond. But even in cities, low-lying areas may be subject to flooding by storm-of-the-century downpours. When buying a house, check with local realtors or building inspectors to learn if the area where you will live is subject to flooding.

Aside from investigating the flood history of an area to avoid buying a house that sits on a flood plain, there is little you can do to avoid floods. When a flood threatens, have an evacuation plan to ensure family safety and try to limit damage to the house and its contents.

FLOOD INSURANCE

Before you experience a flood, check with your insurance agent to learn the limits of your home insurance policy. Coverage for flood damage may require a special amendment to your insurance policy, or a separate policy. Be sure your policy is up to date: inflation has driven the cost of replacement for house and furnishings to ever-higher levels, and the increased ownership of expensive electronic gear has also inflated the value of the contents of the home. If your entire wardrobe is lost, the cost of replacement may be shockingly prohibitive. Be sure your insurance coverage reflects the actual replacement value of your possessions.

Most household policies limit the coverage for expensive items such as art, cameras, jewelry, and furs. If you own any such valuables, have your insurance agent attach a rider to your policy for extended coverage. Keep all the receipts for any major purchases, and have expensive items appraised. You may be surprised to learn that luxuries bought many years ago have vastly increased in value.

Finally, make an inventory of every item of personal property. First make a written, room-by-room inventory, along with receipts for the room contents. Then use a still or video camera to do a photo inventory of every room. Be sure that anything of value is visible in the photo or video tape: open closet doors and photograph the contents of the closet. Do this for every room in the house, then store the written inventory and photos or video tape in a safe place outside the house, such as in a safety deposit box, so it cannot be lost in a storm or flood.

SHUT OFF UTILITIES

If predicted flooding will be severe enough that evacuation from the house is necessary, take steps to limit water damage to the house. Shut off the main water valve. This is the gate valve located near the water meter, on the street side of the meter. If you have a well, shut off the valve located either near the water tank or on the supply pipe from the well to the house. This prevents flood water from contaminating your water supply.

To avoid electrical fires or dangerous shocks to family members when you return to the house, pull the main fuse at the fuse box or the main entry panel, or switch off the main circuit breaker. This will shut down all the electrical circuits in the house.

On gas appliances, including the furnace, shut off all standing pilot lights, and shut off the gas main at the meter. Hang a wrench above the meter so it is handy for emergency shut-off. *For safety, don't turn the gas on or replace the main fuse in the electrical panel until the systems have been inspected by the utility companies.* Better

Water Supply

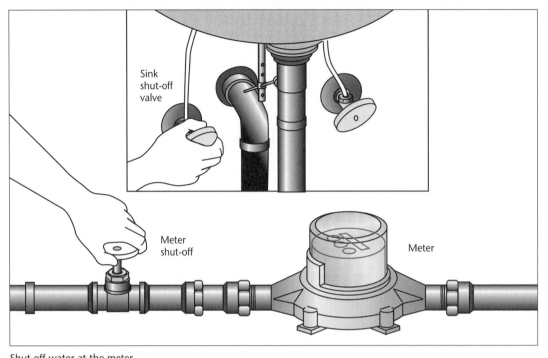

Sink
shut-off
valve

Meter
shut-off

Meter

Shut off water at the meter.

yet, have the utilities turned back on by qualified service-people, after they have conducted professional inspections.

REMOVE FURNITURE

Your first concern should always be family safety, so don't jeopardize human safety to protect property. If time permits, move your most valuable furniture, small appliances, and personal items to an upper floor. If there is no upper floor, stack the most expensive items on tables or on the highest shelves, to try to keep them above the water. For large appliances that cannot be moved, such as the electric range or refrigerator, disconnect the power plugs.

EMERGENCY KITS

If you live in an area that is subject to frequent storms or flooding, don't wait until an emergency has begun to consider emergency equipment. Assemble an emergency kit that contains vital items and can be kept in the car. Items included in the kit may vary depending on the type of storm you expect. A general purpose emergency kit should con-tain a portable radio and extra batteries, a flashlight, blankets or sleeping bags, jumper cables to start the car, candles and matches in a watertight can (to be used for either light or heat), a shovel, and a road map. Also include a first aid kit, along with any prescription medi-cines needed by family members.

Listen to weather updates and move to higher ground well ahead of the flood; don't delay until water covers and conceals the pathway to safety. Don't try to wade or drive through water where you cannot see the bottom; raging water can

Electric Service Panel

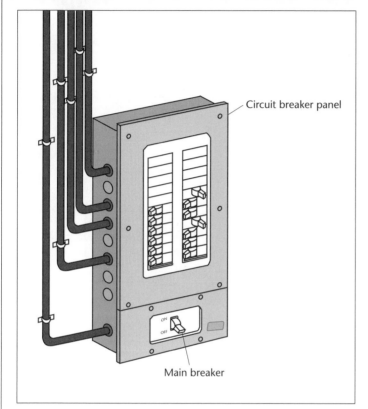

Circuit breaker panel

ON
OFF

Main breaker

Shut off electricity at the service panel. Shown here is a main circuit-breaker shutoff; this may vary. Learn how to shut off your service before an emergency occurs.

penetrated under vinyl floors or soaked into carpets will rapidly deteriorate the carpets and will cause the floors or underlayment to decay). If the carpets or rugs are allowed to dry, and are cleaned, they may be salvageable.

Power-washing the walls and floors of a flooded house is the most effective way to remove mud and dirt.

To clean dirty walls or ceilings, mix 5 tablespoons (75 milliliters) of trisodium phosphate (available at paint stores) with 1 cup (250 milliliters) of bleach into a gallon (4 liters) of warm water. Use a sponge or sponge mop to wash the soiled surfaces, then rinse with clean water. Allow the walls to dry completely before repainting.

After cleaning, the only way to remove so much moisture from the house is by utilizing moisture transfer between the humid indoor air and the dry outside air. Open the windows or remove window sashes to allow fresh air to circulate throughout the house. To maximize air flow, remove storm windows or window screens, and operate portable fans or dehumidifiers. The best way to force air flow is to open all windows and doors, then set fans facing outward near doors or windows on one side of the house. This procedure

wash out roadbeds, so the water may be deeper than you think and currents can wash you or your vehicle away. Head for high ground while you can still see the roadway. Insert "Cleaning Flood-Damaged Interior"

CLEANING FLOOD-DAMAGED INTERIORS

Entering a flood-damaged house can be a shocking experience; the damage done

by water to the house interior and furnishings appears at first sight to be devastating. But, by taking prompt action, the flood damage can be limited.

The first step is to remove all the contents of the house. Store them in the garage, and leave the garage door open for air circulation. If you have no garage, rent storage space. Next, pull up all rugs or carpets and remove them to the outdoors (water that has

Gas Supply

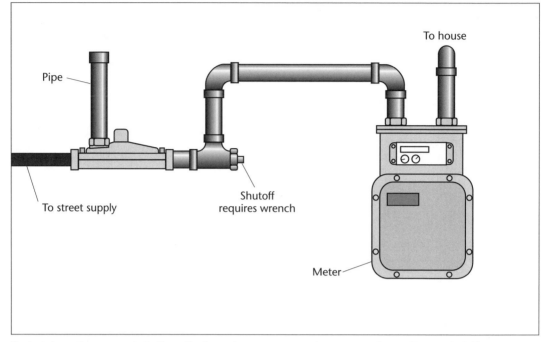

To house

Pipe

To street supply

Shutoff
requires wrench

Meter

To shut down the gas supply to the entire house in an emergency, hang a wrench near the gas shutoff.

provides cross ventilation by pulling air into the house through windows on one side of the house and exhausting it through windows on the opposite side.

If exposed for a prolonged period to standing water, wallboard and plaster can be destroyed. If flood waters recede quickly, and the house is allowed to dry out, these wall and ceiling materials often will be relatively undamaged. Let the surfaces dry completely before you attempt to assess the damage. When the wallboard or plaster is completely dry, push against it with the palm of your hand. If the wallboard or plaster feels soft or spongy under hand pressure, replacement may be necessary. In most cases, ceilings and walls will need minor touch-ups and repairs.

Take apart all locks and hinges on doors or windows. Clean them thoroughly, then apply a light coating of a lubricant such as WD-40 to all moving parts.

Don't be in a hurry to redecorate. New paint may lock residual moisture in the wall or ceiling cavities, causing development of mold, odors, or mildew. The drying time depends on both the extent of the damage and the climate in which you live. Depending on the seasonal humidity, a drying period of six months may be required before the interior is dry and is ready for redecoration.

CLEANING FLOOD-DAMAGED APPLIANCES

When you return to a house that has been damaged by a flood, **do not try to restore electric power yourself.** Have the electrical system and appliances inspected by a qualified service person. Switches and

Gas Appliance Valve

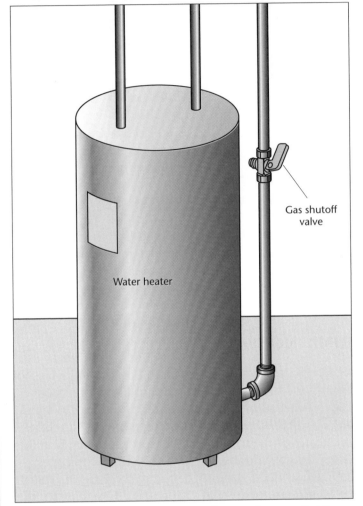

Water heater

Gas shutoff valve

A gas service shutoff valve is located near all gas appliances so that the appliance can be serviced without shutting down the entire house. If a flood is imminent, shut off the main supply at the meter.

have sealed motors and may survive flooding. However, you should have their electrical components, such as thermostats and relays, checked by an electrician. If the water has penetrated the insulation in the refrigerator, lingering odors may make it necessary to replace the appliance. To repair other appliances or tools with electric motors, such as saws, blenders, or food processors, remove the motors and take them to an appliance repair shop for cleaning and service.

CLEANING FLOOD-DAMAGED FURNITURE

Because of the absorbent padding or fill in mattresses, upholstered furniture, and pillows, it is difficult to remove moisture, odors, or bacteria from these furnishings. In most cases these items must be discarded after a flood.

Furniture made of manufactured wood such as plywood or particle board will likely deteriorate and be permanently damaged by water exposure. However, if handled properly, most solid wood furniture can be salvaged. Home insurance policies do not cover flood damage. Check with your agent before you have a loss. You may be able to buy a flood insurance policy

other electrical devices that have been flooded can be wet and can short out or inflict a painful or dangerous shock to family members. Have the service person turn the power on after a complete inspection and when the service has been approved for use.

With the power main shut off, remove, disassemble, and clean light fixtures and lamps before using them. Water can enter cracks in power cords, so replace the power cords on floor or table lamps.

Major appliances such as refrigerators and freezers

available through the government in the U.S.

To salvage solid wood furniture, first use warm water, a detergent, and a scrub brush to remove any mud or dirt. Next, use Borax dissolved in hot water to remove any mold from the furniture, following the directions on the Borax box for the proper mix proportion. Remove the doors and drawers from furniture such as dressers or cabinets, and arrange them so that there is space between them to permit full air circulation to dry the wood. A good approach is to place the doors and drawers so they lie flat and rest on sawhorses, so air can circulate around all sides.

Never move wood furniture into sunlight to dry, because the direct heat of the sun may dry the wood too quickly and cause it to warp, twist, or crack. Dry the furniture indoors, with windows and doors open for cross ventilation. Running a dehumidifier will help dry the wood.

If white water spots or film develop on the wood finish, mix ½ cup (125 milliliters) of warm water with ½ cup (125 milliliters) of household ammonia. Soak a clean cloth in the ammonia/water solution and wipe it over the white areas. Repeat if necessary until the white spots are gone. Allow the furniture to dry completely.

Do not be in a hurry to wax the wood. Allow the wood to dry completely, then use 4/0 (fine) steel wool to apply a liquid wax/polish. When the wax has dried, buff the furniture with a soft dry cloth.

DRINKING WATER

Floods or major storms may interrupt or contaminate the drinking water supply. There may be potable water in the water heater or the toilet tank if they have not been submerged in flood water. If flood water has not entered the freezer, you can melt ice cubes to get water for drinking or cooking.

If no drinking water is available, you can boil water to purify it. To purify the water, bring it to a rolling boil for five minutes. Let the water cool, then pour it rapidly back and forth between two containers. This will aerate the water, help remove odors, and improve the taste of the water.

You can buy water purification tablets at most drug or camping supply stores. If you have no purification tablets, use plain bleach (containing no detergents or additives) to purify the water. Four drops of bleach will purify 1 quart (1 liter) of water; ¼ teaspoon (1 milliliter) will purify 1 gallon (4 liters), and 1 teaspoon (5 milliliters) of bleach will purify 5 gallons (20 liters) of water. Mix the bleach/water solution completely and let it stand for 30 minutes before drinking the water to be sure all bacteria are killed.

Glossary

A

Air-entrained—Concrete that has been combined with chemical additives. The additives make the concrete more dense and resistant to moisture penetration, and also reduce damage to the concrete from freezing temperatures.

Argon gas—Gas that has a higher R-value than air. Argon gas is injected between two panes of glass to decrease heat loss through window units.

Asphalt coating—Coating that is applied to the exterior surfaces of concrete basement walls to seal them against moisture penetration.

C

Chimney effect—Reference to the fact that hot air rises. Cool air entering the attic from soffit vents rises and rises as it warms in the attic, then exits through high-level or ridge vents.

Circuit breaker—Electrical device that is used to replace the old fuse system in electrical wiring. When a fault occurs in the electrical system the circuit breaker switches off to stop current flow through the circuit.

Condensation—Occurs when moisture-laden air meets a cold surface and condenses to become water.

Cornice—A board which finishes off the roof overhang on a gable roof.

Cove—Concrete troweled to form a 45-degree angle at the joint where the concrete basement wall meets the footing below. The cove is designed to shed water away from the joint.

Curtain drain—A drainage trench to disperse water. A drain pipe is placed at the bottom of the trench, then gravel is poured into the trench, up to a level several inches below the ground level. Then black dirt is added and sod is laid so the drainage ditch is concealed.

Cricket—A pyramid–shaped metal device that is installed behind the chimney on the high side of the roof slope. The cricket diverts roof water around the chimney and prevents water from pooling at the joint where the roof and chimney meet.

D

Double-hung—Term that describes a style of window in which the upper and lower units can be opened and closed by moving the units up or down in their channels.

Downspout—The rain gutter member that carries water from the horizontal rain gutter to the ground.

Drain pipe—Perforated plastic pipe that is buried in the ground at footing level, or in the bottom of a drainage ditch to catch and divert water away from the foundation or drainage ditch.

Dry rot—Term that describes rot or deterioration of wood members due to water exposure.

E

Elbow—A device used to change the direction of flow on a rain gutter system.

Fascia—Horizontal wood trim used to finish and enclose the ends of the rafter tails at the roof overhang or soffits.

F

Filter fabric—Fiberglass fabric or mesh that is used to cover underground drain pipes. The fabric permits water to flow through, but stops soil from washing down and plugging the perforations in the drain pipe.

Footings—The concrete slab that supports the weight of the foundation or basement walls. The foundation must always rest on undisturbed soil to prevent settling that occurs in loose-fill soil.

G

Grade—The slope of land is called the grade.

Ground pipe—The horizontal rain gutter member that carries water from the bottom of the downspout to a point away from the foundation.

H

Heat exchanger—An appliance through which runs an exhaust pipe and a fresh air intake pipe. As the warm stale air passes out, heat is transferred to the incoming cold fresh air. The device thus permits fresh air to be exchanged for stale air in the house, while retaining the desired heat.

M

Mildew, mold—Fungi which thrive in conditions where heat, moisture and decay exist. Mildew spores can be killed by chlorine bleach; wash away with water and detergent.

O

Oxalic acid—Acid that is available in crystal form at most paint centers. Oxalic acid is mixed with water to bleach wood that has been darkened by moisture exposure.

P

Parge coat—A 50-50 mix of cement and fine sand. The parge coat is trowelled over the concrete block foundation wall to provide a barrier to water entry.

Percolation—The rate at which soil absorbs water: the percolation rate varies greatly depending on type of soil, ie, sandy, loam, clay, etc.

Perm factor—The rate at which moisture can pass through a building member or material.

R

Rain gutters—Plastic or metal troughs which catch and transfer water from the roof to a disposal area.

Retaining wall—A wall of brick, stone or wood built to prevent soil erosion at the point where the grade level changes. The wall must permit water to pass through while retaining the soil in place.

Ridge—the apex or highest point where two roof planes meet. Also, ridge vent, a ventilator which permits stale hot air to be exhausted from the attic while preventing water entry.

S

Sealer—A paint-like material applied to masonry surfaces to reduce moisture entry through the wall, etc.

Skylight—A window that is installed through the roof to permit entry of light and, if operable, air. When improperly installed and flashed the skylight can be a source of roof leaks.

Slope—The rise or fall of a surface such as a roof or the land.

Soil percolation—See Percolation, above.

Splash block—A plastic or concrete device that is placed on the ground below a gutter downspout. The splash block serves a dual purpose: it prevents soil erosion from the water flow while also directing the water away from the foundation.

Strainer—A dome-shaped wire device that is installed in the gutter at the point where the downspout hole occurs. The strainer prevents leaves and roof debris from entering and clogging the downspout.

Sump, sump pump—A catch basin to collect water from soil drain pipes. The collected water is picked up by a sump pump and transferred to a disposal point away from the house structure.

Swale—A shallow ditch or depression in the soil, created to divert water to a new path around and away from the house structure.

T

Transit—An optical device that is mounted on a tripod. The surveyor peers through the eyepiece at a calibrated surveying stick held by an assistant, to check the lay or slope of the land.

V

Valley—The juncture at which the roof changes direction or plane. The flashing used to waterproof this juncture is called valley flashing.

W

Water table—The point in the earth at which the soil is continuously wet. The first step in finding the source of basement water is to check with your building department to learn the depth of the water table.

Whole-house ventilation—This type of ventilation employs a large-capacity fan to exhaust warm, dry air from the house interior into the attic, where it is removed via roof or ridge vents.

Window well—A u-shaped device made of fiberglass or metal, that is placed around a basement window that is below grade. The units permit basement windows to be below the ground level while providing sunlight and fresh air to enter the basement.

Index

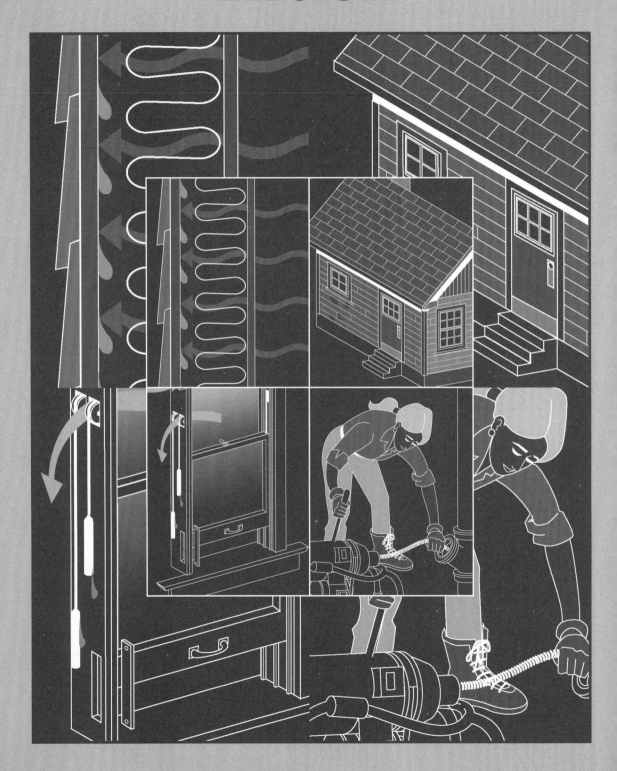

Page citations in **boldface** below refer to **illustrations**.

A

air barriers. *See also* vapor barrier, 68–69
air-entrained concrete. *See* concrete, air-entrained
American Society of Home Inspectors (ASHI), 7
American Ventilation Association (AVA), 87
argon gas, 131
asphalt coating, **14**, 131
attics
    access doors to, 103
    condensation in, 65

B

basements
    moisture sources in, **11**, 11–13
    wall construction of, **14**
bathrooms, vapor control in, 64
bathtub leaks. *See* shower leaks
Beaver Basement Water Control system, 41
Becker, Norman, 7
building inspectors, 7, 13, 15
building materials, moisture content of, 75

C

caulking. *See also* sealers; sealing, 27–28, 35–37, **36**, **81**, 96, 114, **115**
ceilings, sealing of, 65, **66**
cement, hydraulic 40
chimney effect, 53, 69, 131

chimneys, leaks and, **57**
circuit breaker, 131
climate, moisture control and, 7
compacting machines, 28
compaction. *See* soil setting
The Complete Book of Home Inspection, 7
concrete. *See also* cement; waterproofing
    air-entrained, 42, 131
    contractors for, 28–29
condensation, 131
    humidity and, 82–83
    susceptibility to, **86**, 93, 111
    water damage and, 61–62
conservation. *See* water, conservation of
cornice(s), 131
cove(s), **14**, **38**, 42, 131
crawl spaces. *See* ventilation, of attics and crawl spaces
cricket(s), **57**, 58, 132
curtain drain(s), **32**, 132

D

dampness indoors. *See also* humidity, 73
dehumidifying the home, 65, 87–88
desiccants, 84
diffusion (of water vapor), 61
dishwashing, reduced water use during, 120–21
doors
    garage, 103
    insulated, 102
    patio, **101**, 102
    weatherproofing and, 99–100, **100**
downspout(s), 132
drain pipe, 11, 13, 132